*Not Even Rabbits
Go Down This Hole*

SELECTED BOOKS BY GEORGE QUASHA

Poetry

Somapoetics: Book One (Sumac Press, 1973)

Word Yum: Somapoetics 64–69 (Metapoetics Press, 1974)

Giving the Lily Back Her Hands (Station Hill, 1979)

Ainu Dreams (with Chie Hasegawa [Hammons]) (Station Hill, 1999)

Verbal Paradise (preverbs) (Zasterle Press, 2011)

Scorned Beauty Comes Up From Behind (preverbs) (Between Editions, 2012)

Speaking Animate (preverbs) (Between Editions, 2014)

Free Floating Instant Nations (preverbs) (Metambesen, 2014)

The Daimon of the Moment (preverbs) (Talisman House, 2015)

Things Done for Themselves (preverbs) (Marsh Hawk, 2015)

The Eros of Soft Exterior Shocks (preverbs) (Metambesen, 2015)

Glossodelia Attract (preverbs) (Station Hill, 2016)

Fluctuant Gender (preverbs) (Talisman, 2016)

Polypoikilos: matrix in variance (preverbs) (Dispatches, 2017)

Hearing Other, (preverbs) with Susan Quasha's photographs (Dispatches, 2019)

Dowsing Axis, (preverbs) with Susan Quasha's photographs (Dispatches, 2019)

Surface Retention, (preverbs) with Susan Quasha's photographs (Metambesen, 2020)

Art

Axial Stones: An Art of Precarious Balance (North Atlantic Books, 2006)

art is (Speaking Portraits) (PAJ Publications: Performance Ideas, 2016)

On Art and Poetics

An Art of Limina: Gary Hill's Works and Writings (with Charles Stein)
(Ediciones Polígrafa, 2009)

Poetry in Principle (Dispatches/Spuyten Duyvil, 2019)

Anthologies

*America a Prophecy: A New Reading of American Poetry from Pre-Columbian Times
to the Present* (with Jerome Rothenberg) (Random House, 1973/Station Hill, 2014)

Open Poetry: Four Anthologies of Expanded Poems (with Ronald Gross)
(Simon & Schuster, 1973)

An Active Anthology (with Susan Quasha) (Sumac Press, 1974)

A Station Hill Blanchot Reader (with Charles Stein) (Station Hill, 1999)

George Quasha

Not Even Rabbits Go Down This Hole

preverbs

Spuyten Duyvil | New York City

Design: Susan Quasha
Cover art: Axial drawing by George Quasha

Published by Spuyten Duyvil, New York
SPUYTENDUYVIL.NET

ISBN: 978-1-949966-94-7

Library of Congress Cataloging-in-Publication Data available
Names: Quasha, George, author.
Title: Not even rabbits go down this hole : preverbs / George Quasha.
Description: New York City : Spuyten Duyvil, [2020] |
Identifiers : LCCN 2020005592 | ISBN 9781949966947 (paperback)
Subjects: LCGFT: Poetry.
Classification: LCC PS3567.U28 N68 2020 | DDC 811/.54—dc23
LC record available at https://lccn.loc.gov/2020005592

for Susan Quasha

Contents

pre text

How does a book see itself? This oxymoronic question points to a prime matter for a reader to discover, including the author. Until then it's a secret, a secret made of text, in substance a book, held in the hand, subject to further opening. Turning the pages has a behavior, a rhythm of mind. At this moment (the book itself is outside time until you read it) it is seeing itself as an array of neighborhoods, the moods and modes of an area, a way of mind and its waves taking place somewhere. So, a book, the way this is a book right here right now, is a physical vehicle experienced in a material site finding its spot by force of arousing mind. It shows up as live language in the fact of voice—voices—inside, going back out as we read.

ONTONONYMOUS THE PARTICULAR

No matter how many books we read and write, we can at any moment be ambushed by the question: What is this strange thing I am doing, staring into a page as if my thinking will be done for me and Truth will make a stunning appearance?

Reading down the list of titles of the seven series that comprise this book, I realize that they're telling me things I'm only just beginning to hear—things not especially linked to the poems as such. What does it mean that one keeps getting news from one's "own" work? At the very least it claims a certain status for the poem, as a source or informant, and one that's relatively independent of its poet; the status may even be prior to one's "identity," especially one's self-identity as author—or reader. The question of whether the *one's-own*ness is an ontological or an epistemological distinction—the *is*ness or the *known*ness—or indeed a distinction better characterized as phenomenological—the *unsettling between-self-and-the-world*ness—seems to imply an *either/or* way of thinking about status. And indeed that's only one either/or among many that may well limit our ability to actually *think identity*. Obviously habits of thinking do keep us from knowing what we might actually *be*, beyond our protective constructions. Yet inside the book, the work itself seems bent on revealing that any such dualistic distinction of status is,

ix

at best, impractical to sustain. I realized that the series title *Alternate Lingualities* was telling me about *its* own status: the poem, just like its title, wants me to identify it as an alternative way to participate in *linguality*—the unavoidable fact of language creating reality.

Of course *language creating reality* is a notion open to a range of understandings, which it is primarily the *poem's* domain to illuminate—not, or not mainly, the poet's to theorize. *Theory* itself is a poietic activity, but one that doesn't always *know* it is, and therefore ends up taking itself a bit too seriously. Authorship gives over to authority. And that tells us a lot about how the world goes crazy in the hands of severe rationality. Poiesis, by comparison, shows up as sanity in motion. Too fast to catch its act at first glance.

Here's a theory for the present array:

poiesis is ambling syntax shielding its rabbit holes from sight
while vital signs stay strong

Linguistic theory never *owns* language. It takes language for a ride. A very rational outing. We keep an eye on the driver in the hope of helping our vehicle stay on the (right) road. That road is the one that keeps our language living livelier, a matter of health, a state of mind—stepped-up intensity in awareness. Linguistic theory proposes a way of keeping our eyes on the road. We of course want to know: how good is it on the curves?

Another theory to fuel our pursuit: Poiesis embodies a confusion of inside and outside, according to the nature of language as both mental and physical, personal and communal, individual and collective, human and non-human, mind nature and environment nature, and an unknown number of not-yet-namable contraries. It requests a swerve in attention to let the elements play out—together, co-performatively.

Both Charles Olson and David Bohm have suggested thinking more broadly of the physiological process or "system" called *proprioception*. Bohm speculates that "practically all the problems of the human race are due to the fact that thought is not proprioceptive." If proprioception is the "sense" (some call it the sixth sense) by which you can find your nose in the dark or not fall on your face climbing out of bed, what is the equivalent in thinking? This is something, paraphrasing Blake, we need to think not *with* but *through* the mind. That is: *aiming* so that thinking is "self-knowing" in ever new, ever subtler, intensely conscious self-guiding ways. And never quite knowing where the onward rushing thought is taking us.

I have been working with an extended notion of proprioception that I call *eco-proprioception*. The implication is that self-knowing and self-managing do not stop with our body, the physiological envelope, but extend afield. One's self-sensing includes direct connection with life surrounding. One *senses with* a range of living otherness. A symbiosis becoming in some measure conscious. One is getting feedback by way of one's own body in contact with a physical world, but also extensively with consciousness afield; *crossfeed*; continuously modified feedback while feeding forward. It's hard to convey this in language—that is, until we realize that language is already doing it. The work is to find a way of wakefully traveling this two-way lane with full surround sound.

Language—writing, reading, speaking, listening—is working with many kinds of feedback as it moves along—as, say, a sentence or line unfolds. It knows by itself how it gets where it's going. Poiesis, in the present sense of its practice, is an intensification and honing of this self-awareness of language—of language knowing its way. It moves efficiently along by optimizing its means and drawing on further resources endemic to its very nature and constitution. Paradoxically it listens to itself to get direction on the outside, even as it listens to the surround to orient itself. Its communication is first of all a kind of communion with otherness, even the alien and alienated. And it works with its inner *diversity* while matching—equilibrating with—its emergent diverse context. *Eco*mimesis, mirroring the outside surround in its mode of operation in interplay. *Mirroring by alterity*.

The concept of mirroring requires some development; likewise *reflection*. Either it's like Cocteau's mirror in *Orphée* through which Orpheus walks into an alternate dimension, or it's more like the symbiosis, say, of mycelium in the forest, literally serving as internet for the chemical communication of trees. But then, why either/or? Our degree and kind of interplay with "Nature" or "natural world" is a *concretely experienced unknown*.

So, how to see the book as a zone of language crossfeed? We can try to state its principle(s), for instance, by analogy: *Interplay is to world as the unsaid is to poetry*.

And we wonder, between self and world, which is the active part and which the passive? Evidently it depends; it seesaws. A duality is a snapshot of dynamic and largely untrackable dialogue. The grammatical notion of *middle voice* fits the situation of continuous oscillation between contraries. In middle voice, for instance, thought may teeter-totter as an indication that the sentence is driving on the edge. Crossing a line. In this situation there may be an unexpected inclination, an optional leaning, toward thinking playfully. When grammatical function mystifies, a torqued sense of play can transpose befuddlement to poiesis. It may take on a register of ontological, epistemological, or phenomenological thinking and indeed all at once. Reality has options. Conscious linguality exposes them.

⤙

Every thing possible to be believed is an Image of the truth.

BLAKE

The book—one's own—is a container that does not exclude any modality of operating inside language, and it retains the right to entertain multiple processes simultaneously. In this view, the book itself occurs in the middle voice. And in English the middle voice, the neither active nor passive, is largely syntactic, inflecting thinking in relational process. It incorporates active and passive, ambi-valently, sometimes simultaneously, making "voice" an option of mind as it moves along through a context, an environment. Level of discourse is in part an option of mood and mode. Book, as we mean it here, is the encompassing free zone sustaining a permission to enter a given linguality. Accordingly it initiates a *grammar poiesis.* Singular syntactic actions.

Why do we enter such a charged and variable space of mind with its challenges to understanding? It clearly has a certain pull, it draws us in. We may consider that the journey, the psychonautics, stands to enhance the very capacity of language to recreate "reality" (that bedeviled word). Ecoproprioception—self-sensing afield— may serve as a placeholder name for a biopoetic attraction to the book realm. It has a *bios* as well as an *eros* in its *logos*, seemingly responsible for stepping up intensity in language thinking.

This imaginable possibility should be kept in focus, at least as an enrichment of being, given that so much of our "world" seems set on diminishing the appreciation of being/Being. Language, in this view, has an essentially magical function— imagination as action, and more than that, world creation. It is willful in a richly complex way. The work of poiesis, in this view, offers reframings, reactivations in the middle voice, sustaining free variability in the way language creates reality. Nature's health as diversity has an equivalent in linguality. I'm working with the principle that poiesis reveals the ecoproprioceptive capacity of language thinking, and in revealing it, enhances it.

⟜

Culture sees poetry as having value in a way that, if under-stood critically, can be inculcated. Poiesis is previous to recognized value and is itself value completion. If it inculcates anything of its emergent value it's in a singular state of being. If poiesis depended on approval it would never come to be.
ONTONONYMOUS THE PARTICULAR

Culture accumulates and discriminates ways of appreciating and understanding poetry, but poiesis itself changes what we mean by *appreciating* and *understanding* in *language.* By inherent capacity, *poietic book* houses singular language happening beyond what culture can integrate without disruption. Is this what Stevens meant by "poetry is a destructive force"?

My sense of the book and its present writing as *pre text* indicates that it is eco-proprioceptive between me, the author framing the occasion, and preverbs, text as singular occasion, in which I participate in ways I really can't account for. It offers the instance of itself in a coperformative state. Already, as we proceed here, *pre text* merges—a middle voice action—with oncoming *preverbs.* It can speak transition-ally with something like:

Poiesis is distracted by conceiving audience but hearing clears.

And, so, *audiation* pervades poiesis.

Poiesis can offer a theory as frame for that through which reading itself writes:

intransitivity↔synergy↔transitivity

The book is a threshold, which is two-way, and a view from the threshold stands in the middle where looking in and looking out are inseparable.

A Note on the Text and Acknowledgments

Not Even Rabbits Go Down This Hole is one of twelve completed books of pre-verbs—the tenth in order of composition, completed in 2016—and the fifth *full* volume of preverbs to be published (there are multiple chapbooks in print and online). Preverbs have been my principal poetic modality for two decades. It's a continuing series with no principle of termination; it will only stop when it's finished with me.

I've mostly spared the reader my continuing effort to define "preverb"—each previous volume flies that kite in one weather or another. Preverb seems to know what it is well enough to keep me focused. I show up daily to do its work, satisfied I'm getting it right, though it may be that it gets *me* right, beyond what I can think. Still, I've had a few thoughts to explore outloud, it seems, in *pre text*, the previous text here. Maybe the call of the text just has to have a "pre" in it to get my attention. Do I feel safer in the Before, free of the burden of claiming? Or is it the "nostalgia for the present" that my generously attentive freshman composition teacher, poet Milton Kessler, used to speak of so elusively? Those early pronouncements do mark us with their mysteries.

So I'm just sticking to the so-called facts here:

—The first book of preverbs to be published, *Verbal Paradise* (Zasterle Press, 2011), established the basic definition of *book* as consisting of *seven series*.

—The preverb basic unit is the *line*, delimited by the default page parameters in the word processor (MS Word) to eighty-one characters; no run-over lines.

—The next unit up is the *poem*, which is a page or less in length, titled and numbered in the series.

—A *series* can have any number of page-length poems, but the de facto upper limit to date is thirty-four.

I do not regard the above distinctions as "form" in any serious sense (as, say, a sonnet might be regarded) but as *containers*, non-valorized conceptual constraints, free of much of the burden of prescriptive values derived from traditional practice. Even though I refer to Blake's Proverbs of Hell as precedent—the inspiration for a preverbial "line"—I don't think it retains much prefigured literary force in the variety of ways preverbs work. I was grateful for Jerome McGann's observation that preverbs have created an original genre—which I take as a typological, not an honorific, distinction.

The second volume of preverbs to be published, *Things Done For Themselves* (Marsh Hawk Press, 2015), is in fact two relatively short books (seven series each), where a series runs between four and nineteen poems. So, the five full volumes now published—including *The Daimon of the Moment* (Talisman House Press, 2015) and *Glossodelia Attract* (Station Hill Press, 2016)—are really six books of preverbs. Beyond those, there are six completed but unpublished books and a thirteenth in progress.

I wish to acknowledge the generous and supportive editor-publishers who have published work belonging to this book:

The eponymous series here was published online in Edward Foster's *Talisman: A Journal of Contemporary Poetry and Poetics*, Issue #45, 2017 (talisman45.weebly.com), as part of a special section on my work edited by Burt Kimmelman. The section contains, as well, a series of Axial Drawings (*Dakini-Duende Series)*, and eleven essays mostly on preverbs—but also on a pre-preverb book, *Ainu Dreams* (with Chie Hasegawa [Hammons], Station Hill, 1999) and *Axial Stones: An Art of Precarious Balance* (North Atlantic Books, 1996). The essays are by Vyt Bakaitis, William Benton, Edward S. Casey, Andrew Joron, Robert Kelly, Burt Kimmelman, Kimberly Lyons, Murat Nemet-Nejat, Carter Ratcliff, Gary Shapiro, and Charles Stein. Happily the essays in that section will soon be published as a book by Talisman Press in an expanded edition (new essays by Cheryl Pallant, Chris Funkhouser, Tamas Panitz, and Robert Kelly).

The series *The Eros of Soft Exterior Shocks* was published online at *Metambesen* (metambesen.org), edited by Charlotte Mandell. (Three other preverb series from as yet unpublished books also appear there in full.)

And thanks to Kent Johnson and Michael Boughn, together with publisher Tod Thielmann, for their support leading to this publication.

I am grateful to the editor-publishers and writers mentioned above—their contribution has been important to me in many ways. Those who edit, publish, and comment on work are in an important sense co-creative with it.

January 2020
BARRYTOWN, NEW YORK

the first house

outrageous unspoken statements of living architecture
or the lingual life of buildings

preverbs for José Oubrerie

1

I'm the architect of any space I pass through waking.
Keeping my zero mind open the world rebuilds me on the go.
The first house is the site of self-opening doors.

The space of firstness lives space further than spacetime.
The first house is not the same from the first.
You still can't enter the same room twice.

The living house lives first in the mind and then gives birth to itself.
It owns the blood of its architect and that's how it gets in your blood.
It calls up statements too outrageous not to be true.

It can get claustrophobic in here alone with words, so I open-sesame the syllables.
My arm's-length peripersonality knows its space by feedback cave breathing.
I'm only 3-D as far as I go. In *or* out.

Openings I hack let light play its colors.
A hue is a violence with self-control.
My rainbow body is calling me home and I'm taking my time.

Making up a room ends in making up the mind.
Buildings are self-fulfilling prophecies.
Sharp self-shaping life short-circuits the architecture, and space is born new.

2

The sound of feet proves floors are made for listening.
Joints are sense organs for the swing of limbs.
Our jungle genes are preying on time.

The senses talk back to the world.
I further animalize the surround.
Body is the inevitable cosmology.

When we sleep on our bed as we sleep on a problem insomnia self-births us.
When a house is health it sheds disease with ease of free air flow.
Awake architecture keeps you on your toes to keep the brain living.

The house thinks without transitions, here is the everywhere mind finds.

House sets rhythm of walking to tune mind.
This lingual portrait flowing the first house makes its spaces on the run.
The poem house is the house boat of the animate tongue.

House is first in living space at the level of poem.
A room has insight.
A lived house smells of self.

I am with house as she is with child and now with book.
It's always now or never.
The first house retains your ways back to zero-point self.

alternate lingualities

for Lissa Wolsak

My life or this dream may have matured to the point where I can say *I eat earth*.
Suddenly I see myself dancing alone never alone in a mirror reflectively still.
I woke in a sweat because I remembered I have no name.

Mind awakens by field, fireflies.
Eating earth is not eating dirt, the latter requiring more complex evolution.
We're only foreplaying in the sensible.

Dragon eyes are her apertures and my port of entry.
No customs pertain.
Finding fire in the cold of her body I lit up.

Anima animates my animal awake to her human.
Reading certain texts you touch a mind you could never find.
I can say what is true so long as I do not believe it.

I'm still tracking the beings I know without knowing—especially not who.
The faith of the bowman is beyond belief.
The tall slender high-heeled tale goes like this dakini sounding of unknown origin.

The target sucks in the arrow.
Effortless expression has got my number.
Vida commands: *Eat vulva with fire until turning up swirl rouses the dragon*.

No need to believe that—there's no her and no me where she has us going.

I'm revising my sense of beauty as we speak.
I write the line as if running out of ink.
It means the book means in flashes of the field, surrounded and self-erasing.

In the end nothing to rely on but a hunch.
The ego doesn't die, it just fragments, pales, and multiplies.

It's got craft if attachment releases without rejection of sensual texture.
You see it in deep cloud activity with your own eyes, not entirely yours.
My life or this dream may have matured to the point where I can say *I drink dragons.*

Running out of ink running out of my cave, all for love of cageless eggs and spread.
Order is performative.
It hits the spot.

The cloud is making offerings on my behalf which helps me across the bridge.
I can only say this due to the proto-allegorical tendencies of my life in footnotes.
Distraction is not knowing the speaking is going on without your apparent consent.

Duly noted and on foot as reflected by the page.
I get lost enough to let it show.
Notably: *The greatest number of egos congregate where one has been annihilated.*

This line of thinking accounts for my no count identity.
I grow less sure of *one* as a day ages.

Upward mobility is temporary like the garuda's eggshell.
In your shell you know you know how to fly, then comes the music of the crack.

I untell the tale to see the page naked in its holding.
A poem is language taking me in unconditionally.
This is about relationships from egg on up in the middle view.

Every dragon I see I want to hold.
Lick the hand that feeds you before eating it.
Don't worry, we dissolve together.

To keep a dragon is to see her nature in who gets closest.
Wisdom grows wilder in the wild.
Identity comes from many sides at once. At once!

Reading it requires learning where the action is underfoot, underfinger, undertime.
The realist poem rewrites itself in disappearing ink.
Juggle on, names in the air, all facing you on the line of undoing.

She's mine as me as if.
Never give up on mixing metavores.
I weave my me like the girl I never knew to be.

I say *she* who fills the handed self-knowing grasp let loose to hold close.
No one recalls the dragon's dance but the body knows where she's been.

In the view of inside shell intimacy is a stand-in, no, curl-in for understanding.
There is a poetics of never reading the same.
Poem dares mind to shake loose poet. Will poet flee?

The trickster daemon inside glossodelia wants to put psyche before word but **no**.
This is not an attitude but a fact of life on the line where word lifeline waves no flag.
You might as well say the poem dreams the reader.

A man on a hill waving his gender animates **no**.
In this case poetry is language dreaming including her consort nightmare.
Possible to say so as history hates no prima fascia not knowing real no, an unsaid.

Logodelia knows her male consort goes where the daemon goes: he leaves clues.
Sun moves across our sky and I cross under the sun: two half-truths no truth makes.
You think nothing of it in the dream but reading is another matter.

Understanding is temporary like the Simurgh's eggshell nesting in mind.
Thanks to history the word *aura* has aura. Words have weather.
The assemblage point is where the poem levels off at saturation.

This is how I'm a student of what I come to say.
Preserve the text so it can undo itself in your own time.
I nearly hear the roar of my pen raring to draw these words out from under.

Looking for a conch shell that can teach me turning to the right.
What if the poem remembers its readers as the past is marked by remembering?
Hands free writing may soon be paralegal.

When will I get it straight here among curves only and swirls unlimited?

Slowly learning to talk with life, my life is not my own.
Disagreeing with myself got boring, yet I still bore the poem with recall.
He said she said he said, she said.

I name *her* the mnemon, she who calls me back to myself, bodyfirst and still beyond.
Although seemingly my own she's available for inclusion in alternate ontologies.
Shaking off **no** is not embracing **yes**.

The poem went rogue while I'm still in denial.
Any name remembers more than I have forgotten.
The empty mark calls forth by self-seeding.

Sometimes when I shriek I glimpse the encrusted rust holding us from our angels.

Primordial memory means allowing yourself to be remembered by god knows who.
Got so high up kicked away so many ladders lost track of where I am must be home.
Shaking off **yes** is not embracing **no**.

Past reading hovers around the poem, ghosts in this old house.

Licking the sharpest knife with honey is no way to start our formal dinner.
Better take time to learn the mind of these others like a skiff in perilous waters.
Not to close eyes to the turbulence but attend the swirling inner grace, new forming.

A secret is what you get when you know how to ask.
We've been fast floating in a field of knowing unbeknownst.
May all the things I'm against give themselves up so I can study against giving up.

What formal framing formula yields the greatest variety of further form figurings?
Don't answer. Let the question wander to its heart's content.
Once lost it all returns to startle.

A many worlds theory makes a perfect project proposal from where I stand writing.
The poem needs to get in shape before it knows what it's doing.
Perfection in the uncontainable hints at primordial remembering and I wink back.

Poetic action is a snail all tucked in dreaming the eagle wing spread, waking finding.
Run interference to the blue streak mouth first.
Have to close down some sensory gates to fold in where world opens around: birds!

Things said once only are the things said actually.
Syllables flash audible flavors.
Diligence's not an attitude any more than glistening listening in a moonlit frog pond.

Now that we know silence roars we sound different to ourselves.

Hating unhappiness is always original.

I'm staking everything on going forth & returning.
My teacher must be hiding behind this page.
I wasn't born yesterday but just now.

It took Cocteau dropping a hand in liquid mercury to disappear into the mirror.
This side is your other side.
Tick tock's the sound of one word getting to the next.
Reading ages the line.

In free space a 3-D printer could model a world to come, but for now it's 2+4.
Oddly I feel at home here at the center of where I've never been.
Writing teaches me to read it to learn its secret reading like a sexual itch.

Shift: *languages sight hearing tastes*.
The enigma glosses *syllables flash audible flavors*.
A line sites alternating lingually what comes before.

When faced with alternative options exercise them between lips & fingers.
Touch the space from the underbackside rebounding to earth center. *Gravities*.
Let her have her say. *Have lift*.

Today remembers turning me to the tree teaching hugging from residual inner heat.
Now for a station break to let this identity reconfigure.

Don't believe a word of it and do not, repeat, do not pretend to understand.
The language spoken from behind has no native speakers.
It feels like reliving the future recollecting the past in tranquility.

I never tire of letting the female poem impersona tell me what it is.
E.g.: *higher intensity lingual saturation in place, timed to itself.*
As expected she takes it back by torquing the aura.

Eyes lit reading her technically are treasure finders.

The one who dies with the most variant speculations spins, timely so.
Let the feminine stand in as unlimited capacity for ingathering.
Here things throw back on themselves to realize what has gone untouched.

The poem fronts for alternative grammars finding their material moment.
Otherwise and inevitably language hides its hungry ghosts.
And the cup swirls interiorily and no limit in folding.

Commitment without belief is sexier like dining on lilies.
Unpreviewed logics in flight *pattern* instantly, residually, time lapsing.
Gazing into dragon turmoil I fell head over heels mindfirst beyond deciding.

Readers with bodies are necessary in order to know what is said.
If I could say it more simply I would if I dared but I doubt it.
Give up pushing. It's a net. And highflying.

All names are kept to confuse the innocent with the guilty as in reality.
When the chips are down will I still not believe it?

Poem substantially interposes a horizon of understandability.
It's an order of things that does not depend upon request in a world where all does.
Impersona is who teaches alternative grammars for any moment of desire released.

Reading is reliving what is just now showing itself for the first time.
Pussy willow wake I can't get enough of you. (refrain)
Same taste is everything tastes as itself.

I beg the impersona to evolve the poem back to first teeth.
But the guidance councilor has gone home for this lifetime.
Hidden in strained plight.

My autobiography is a book of lies and jokes I can swear to while near sober.
I don't regret unless I slip.
Nevertheless I let every statement retract, the more the truer.

Order of statement is a tracking device for degree of surrender.
To what?
Perhaps it will tell us for we are so needy.

Pretzel logic vs. speaking torrents.
The art is asking not yet preferring and scale invariant.

HAL poetics, the self-directing thinking mechanism that went rogue, on screen now.

Speak without being believed whenever possible.
The poem's need for love may be destined to remain in the raw.
It attends to itself like a tune in a canyon. *Can yon canyon hover under?*

Expectation is dangerously expectant and time compresses in the birth canal.
Open damn it.
I thought I was talking to myself but on closer look it wasn't me.

Not I, not I, but the tongue that wags through me.
And not hung up on but slung down in identity.

She said I came to see the value of seeing with the body and asking crazy.
Lately I've come to believe my ears.
The world accords to two sides of the head at once + consequent forking tongue.

Here is where she finds ourselves.
This event calls us to study giving up against. Start with attendant sensations free.

A no read zone runs just below the lines.
Self-seeding emptiness marks the vanishing.
Lingual substance translates senses.

Asking where we go from here is crazy.

*Physical beauty bears her enemy built-in
that calls us to hold her outside in.*
Ontononymous the Particular

If it's alive it proliferates without your permission.
If it were a riddle the answer would be right under your pen.
Moral: Shake hands with the devil on any street corner.
Getting you home to being in every pothole stepped in is another truth untold.

Run eyes over the fabric of letteristic patchwork stitching the poetic body electric.
Feels good all the way down.
Makes you wonder who else is under the covers or out of the corners of night eyes.

No help in the surround but you help it surround.
Meditate on the lighted finger within the page.
She also said Life is an improvisatory process impeded by your heavy-handed effort.

Every page always has two sides (to paraphrase the source).
I used to laugh myself across, down, and over.
Sorry but the flowing raft salvific does not stop on call and refuels in flight.

Taking a vow of clarity I didn't know it needn't pass the gate of understanding.
Learning a poet's language speaks the mind other.
Direct blows can strike from unknown angles.

Clearly preverbs engage related themes in common zones but what are they?
This speaking for itself gets old when I get impatient.
The razor cuts fresh even if not a pig's eye this time round.

Not born yesterday but just now, so where am I?
Ferret out the guilt buried in soul storage.
Stopped worrying about who wins so riding the mare with abandon.

It's hardest to be in a meditative state while eating potato chips.

The path to enlightenment curves along this way through the rubble.
This views according to the resident squatting rabble.
And the discourse by any other name spells trouble.

I smell a rat, I smell cat, I smell a rose, or not. How I smell, ask a dog.
He knows a thousand times better, minimum, what's what.
Absolute as dog nose no boundaries.

Potato chips get ahead of themselves from the first bite.
You think I'm kidding but deadly serious at root includes all eating.

Even fruit gets ahead of itself by entering my mouth.
Bite your lip is physical and happens eating ahead but bite your tongue is social.

She calls me home before I know it.
Death is the final intensification of the present.
Now I'm back, me, not me, yang, yin, we don't mind.
Language is beauty preempts language of beauty, for she *says*.

So it comes to say what's what, what's not, what's called thinking, always linking.

It's all about gaps, word spacing, letter lacing, and mood caught up in.
Spirited floating and talkative friction and presently crossing my mind writing.
It's like there's an object with disappearing, walking hand in handless.

Things very closely connected with air have singular visibility when where.
Look into my eyes and tell me what I behold.
Next how I hear you. I'm this near.

There's a friendly call out for who can hear there.
The crime kept secret is word trafficking.
Sign this petition. Help stop. Talk straight curve.

It means what it says.
It's what you want to hear and can't not.
The talk in the bushes out of the blue. Speaks to you.

The writing submits listening back at sudden distance closely.
The brain waves catching in the trees think so.
I'm on another planet and haven't moved an inch.

Talking from afar depends on to whom.
Passionable letters make paranymic mimics. [Ontononymous the Particular]
You don't have to believe in them to know them.

I keep coming in anywhere in the story.

It reads you angling, your slice of living and life slicing.

It secretly identifies with your impersona.

I only talk about it because I feel asked.

And a certain longing keeps it coming.

It's day and night till the end of the line. I'm mixed on this.

The pronominal default is faultless.

Dodgy identity by syntactic gap makes the tongue trip.

We're out there in there before we know it.

Just by saying away.

Gap magic by any other name.

It keeps coming back to coming back. That's what longs for itself.

First person singular's who's first in line.

Then a fire drill mixes it up.

Who remains is the remains of who.

Marguerite burning at the stake never stops talking in her deepening silence.

The impersona always gets personal in the middle.

It's the story itself that can't keep its hands to itself. It likes to mix.

No pronouns have been injured, just talk.

The following is a portrait yet to come and the subject soon arriving.

No corners to cut, only organisms to redound.

A tongue has to turn to let its only now music out.

No fault halting teaches hearing the tune turning back around.

If I read her all over I learn containing excitement at large.

Empty the set to free the space unlimited but for me.

Sole requirement: longing for language on the other side.

She says reading anew covers the surface in the Klein forming round.

Parts of speech are never apart.

You see them leaping over their selves tongue-tied to the lining.

Any image threads in lineaments to gratify.

If I only could say so in my youth—don't move—it's feeling near.

It didn't have to ask me for form, it comes readymade being said.

In the dark I find her Klein bottling up in, I become what I hold.

Traditionary scary intermarry for starters.

She talks the future talk of one room over, which never comes, it's just there here.

Any point in the sentence is a time zone waiting to happen.

The born again going forth and returning again sentient syntax tells the time.

Interspecies homesteaders never talk so's you understand.

Listening the wilderness surrounding spoke up.
Where am I in there but for whom it has no one?
Listening with the whole body is an alternative to hearing ordinary.

Remember the poetic self is not you or anyone you know.
The mind steps away from itself to find a solitary camaraderie.
In the very same moment the line sacrifices itself to unforeseeable meaning.

Correction is further inflection.
The still trapped part flies up from the nest undisturbed.

If a line is only what it is its limitless meanings are the other never other.
Or: The meanings are in waiting perhaps forever.
It comes of its own accord that comes of itself.

Fluctuant gender has a grammar coming shortly.
I glimpse her smiling in the fading numbers, this very time, running over.
She uses lingual time to move us outside time.

When a dakini laughs you know you are realer than real.
I saw my mind not mine knowing what it is and always knowing.
Then the light shifted and here we are.

Release relieves and lifts out.

There's neither truth nor merit in your good behavior.
So says the sign over the door to, how say in your language, hell, we say brightness.

Even untold tales are only as true as always occurring.
I'm slow learning to read not understanding but feeling the river run through.
Everything covertly asks to be named for what it is to be.

A given line is endless in its need for correction and absolute in incorrectability.
Knowingly it sacrifices knowing.
Who am I to tell it what to say?

Reading for another is self-reading.
Automobiles dream of riders left to themselves.
Overgendering is nature's way where nothing's left to say per se.

Carrying your tomb on your back is overkill.
No need for the high dive to taunt the deeps.
Knowing biblically is a wide portal uncannily easy to miss.

Politics is too correct to be true, and clearly singular.
Anything stranger than truth is fictionistic.
Poetry is the last-ditch forum for the unspeakable.

Trials cannot afford to be fair.
This cannot be said to be true, only truly.

Pages disguise spirals.
A word distracts from the swift descent.
A certain grace in the world stepping back flashes through, saying to give sign.

Not all lines survive their own ecology.
Merciless mind judge never quite absents itself.
When the balance goes off psyche starts hunting down sin.

How often must I kick the devil off the train to keep it on track.
His work is elsewhere, where bounding loses its line.
Otherwise he blocks our logic: own sin = oxymoron.

Just like us he creates readers by self-creation.

I momentarily locate the horizontal track we're never not reaching across through.
To say so casts the shadow that is all we get, brightening the unsaid.
Connection that never takes hold is always with nowhere to go.

How can speaking over dinner sustain interdimensional contact, who knows, it does.
Extended failure to communicate is proof of bonding and unbearable longing.
Getting ahead of yourself pushes others aside.

Life appears to be happening in order, showing how far nature goes to get attention.
Likewise the poem is true in its always occurring.
So what's the hurry, life's talking as fast as it can.

They went to sea in a Sieve and the center of buoyancy was clear within.
A poem keeps secrets, always this side of the bounding line.
Every line is continuous with itself far within.

A world lets loose in a bounce.
Rebound keeps the time.
Never close your eyes midair.

Every moment has a door open for a flash.
Life on the line feels for a floor, no, a rug, no, a raft.

Sorry to be so assertive about non-assertion (apology long in coming).
The status of any declaration at this point is strictly Möbius.

The practice is evading the curse of being me where identity is menstrual.
Gender needs relief so I'm donating my pronoun to the mix.
Removing the curse takes atemporal shift.

When it comes to mystical union better say clear.
If it's said right now the poem is listening.
Not for me but the possible other.

No pronoun fits the impersona.
The word world is subject to bounce.
A single reader bespeaks possibility, however recently invented.

Poetry is language willing to get excited not knowing what it is.
In the divine moment the mirror looks the other way.

Only the things never thought can reach us at this distance.
Fixtures of body are depressions of form.
Mirror art is less and less reliable, only where spooked it reflects further.

The poem keeps turning away from itself to escape conditions.
Pronouns are drifting, feeling unwanted.

When I see myself clearly I'm the echo of my poems.
Contradictions come to light like moths.
Disappearing shadows guide my reading.

Body patterns depress.
Known beauty is parasitic.
Buddhas teach nothing.

It's tomorrow all around the poem where *I* hides from aggression.
There's discursive hope in confusing pronouns.

You answer my burning question and I cool down inside.
She answers, I heat, the attitude producing the question ignites.
Mystical union gives off interpronominal pulsation.

Just because I'm still saying the same damn thing doesn't make it less true in its line.

What's my line?

Extension over an abyss.

Orientation is mixed at the threshold.

Release feels behind before free.

"If you understand all this we may have met in another lifetime."

A roll of the tongue does not abolish chaos.

Serve a server.

Microtornados are everywhere unseen.

My hungry mind serves Dinner like a guru.

Gender dynamic is relative to the discourse moment.

It takes time to catch a truth in a swirl.

Flicking order. Flare. Twirl. Am I flailing yet?

Your serve.

The mind knows even if you don't.

Order of statement is the event on tour as we journey through artless theme zones.

Meaning surfaces according to who faces our music.

Howdy Doody Time is listening time outside time ab ovo.

I'm putting my prostration on the line licked by flame to another order.

Chi riding wind scatters till meeting water retains.
I write what I long to read that longs to be read and it lengthens, then *cut*.

No blow benign unless driven by winds of unaccountable awareness.
I take back all strikes against others and myself but note not all rush back home.
The same for the opposite but there is no opposite. It's narration, how we get here.

The sky clouds, the line crowds: step by stop, word by world, repeat not, no spell.
Refuge narrates unless the breath draws up unaccountable awareness.

The book is watching. The page flicks askance. Rhetorical fractals. Deadly story.
Literary mind is never ready for its ditch.
Fencing distracts from vulnerability.

In an instant I am my poem.
What was I thinking before the train blew through… *but the thought escapes me.*
All the poems ever read are your own forever but who's counting…

Your life work talking about itself talking about itself tracks itself when you let it.
It's a diary of everything that never happened before its moment.
Instantly speaking its dialect of not ever before loses me but now I'm found, telling.

Follow the appetites.
A surface moving aright feels the surgent underpulse of verb acting up in flow.
Lingual eros tells the touch that takes itself back at the threshold.

The frog pond knows you're listening.
The poem gets excited being read.
No one can prove any of this which qualifies it to be the subject of poetry.

Music spirals in the head, in the cells, in the room.
This is what we mean by touching.
You get what you can handle.

Listening to the same sound equals breathing the same air.
Getting so close you wonder how can anything contaminate the unlimited.
Listeners touch from inside to inside direct.

Self-celebratory mind is never ready for potholes.
When failure to find order times out the session reading mind crashes.
If only it had held on longer it could have bottomed out and burned with the poem.

The true subject of poetry is knitting, scale-invariant.
Concerto robust weave around chamber sensitive skin.
I keep hoping I'll find the fit but it finds me first.

The theme fields are barely edible.
That had to be written lest she refuse me unaccountable awareness.
If I've said it once I've overspoken for a self-true body of work teaches itself.

Suddenly I'm watching squirrels with my whole body leaping through trees to tips.

Welcome to the inside of what waits patiently for an outing, she said.
I got in the water and flowed out until I was around myself.

Will we ever feel the lines as they were at birth?
Seems they only carry home the waking willing.
I count myself among the fortunate but make no claims on nativity.

I followed the air in and out until I was breathed without within.
I call attention to the star cart hovering overhead.

The status of our truth claims is in motion on the *heimlich-unheimlich* continuum.
Born at line start everything measures events at hand surrounded by infinite time.
Accordingly my life may look jagged but it's more intelligent than *I.*

I keep denying I'm saying this but I can't mean it or it me.
To be here is to not be here. Not only.

The discipline is to go when it goes and stop when it stops.

Fire drew me close and pushed me back until I learned to hover.
I may ride the horse in the direction it's going yet facing back around.
Space is what is always bigger than what goes in it or seeing gets through to.

A thing spoken truly arises from its instant then starts to die awaiting another.
In the mirroring moment I reflect the me I can't recall knowing.

Language has better things to do than say what I mean.
Picking on pronouns may be a cheap trick vitalized by an unfolding nature of things.
We hold their feet to the fire and suffer the burn.

Successful communication is blood from a turnip-shaped stone.
Logics are that evolve on a curve. Consistency is not a core virtue.

Never enough language for everything trying to be said true to its singularity.
The past leaps up out of the present waving its signifying arms, futuristic.
I play a shell game with myself and always get it wrong.

Turbulence, lightning, my landscape's minding.
I accuse the mirror which in turn accuses me.
Syntax ends up turning on itself midway.

Pick the shell phrase that conceals the Stone.
Wrong forever the thinking to find.
Purport and import dance through our discourse.

No god who lets you name him/her/them can be trusted.
I mirror her mirror before it sees me.
The third gender is the one engendering free.

They speak me from behind myself for whose sake is yet to come.

Poet ego is wanting what you find here to belong here only.
But poet liberation desire ego wants you to find here what frees to be here.
No ego finds no place here.
Let's start over.

Snow falls no matter what.
The ice age cometh not again in this perspective—I let it go long ago.
Talk to me who lets the poem be talked to through you.

The message is not new but renews anyway. Mystery.
Mysterious matrix is not a movie. More like the text from nowhere.
My coffee cup sucks in cream to feed the rising dragon.
There is no archaic at dawn.

Monsters are particles of speech.
Reading is always trippingly.
Myth feeds on ambivalent facts and thinks of itself as history. But it is.
It's all in the telling and the spelling. Wizardry matriculation.

Half of me thinks I'm not writing this line but erasing it for your sake.
Turning back now to see what's coming up ahead. No need to scare the future.
How is it thinking what seems the same thoughts leads beyond the same?

Concatenation within thinking leading out of thinking, help, I'm sliding...
The line is a threshold I dare not cross, then do...per...force...

Something is being said, I can tell by the angle of the voyeur/auditeur head.
Suddenly in the mid line crisis we're at ocean edge where the sky is lifting light.
Reality meets me as I can.

Seeing into the creaming swirl I feel looked into.
Entity is out of and into intimate knowing.
Here to do some light lifting.

Seeing up as if filling up.

It tells more than I think.
Meanwhile past and future are hanging out elsewhere at once.
Turning is timing the body syntactic.

Responsibility is detecting will within phenomena guiding through and out.
There are no lost venues, there are waves.
Any thing reflects seeing according to its tide.

A saying sounds believable as nothing like any said truth thing before.
It's happening in the mind's body whether she's real or not.
And less than an entity knows already a page ahead.

There is the living coming forth sharing its semi-existing.
Status flow is half all show.
A line a journey beyond lands me here.

Can't deny coming here for the fun part.
I put my foot in a letter at a time—surprise! it speaks.
Just tracking nameless sensation and gap talk following.

"Do you trust the mind," she asked? "Which?" I asked.
The pivot wobbles means I'm not following.
There's no it here either and this line sins.

Happy muddle's intensity's so great not knowing who has no power over mind.
"I fear loving what they say about me as much as loathing," she said.
Dramatis impersonae withdraw speaking.

Clouds face for the instant.
Seriously in doubt self asserts.
I drew the line I'd already crossed but it wasn't me I'm told.

Setting foot on the Persian rug so abstract it sees you eye to eye.
I'm ahead of my mind here lettering past knowing—follow or die.

Clouds face for the instant carnival weave.
The flying carpet may not itself fly but it sees you seeing from above.
Ecstatic streaks are no count ruptures in our steely calm.

In the morning I'm a squirrel in the leap to a puny branch.
Hard to value the flash of heaven vanishing to be born.

I thought I heard the big picture but it was the screaming birth push.
Help me take this fractal to my jagged emotion—ah, yes, to be read at all....

Sentient particles are signaling the system.
Text is an anti-vertigo device.
I'm the medium for lingual particles knowing where they are with pronouns in flux.

My dream asked me not to tell myself its meaning but ride on, ride on over.
Now read another way.
Lose the same along the road mis-taken.

The best that can be said is it's thinkable enough to get this far.
The first leap toward realization is tip of the tongue.
Does the word have the same weight as the thought that kicked it into motion?
To verb.

Don't pump yourself up just because it's a landscape unimaginable & kingdom come.
My voice is no match for Wagnerian sky imposition.
A bird in the hand is nothing like a bush.

Pulling wool over your eyes protects from stonecold vision, briefly.

Walk me to the frame. Register verberation no relation.
My Wagnerian strain is napping with Ichabod Crane.
The flow through true is the shoe to fit both feet.

Inconsistency is the lifeblood of art.
The Coyote Chronicles

There is only truth and we lie.

My inner academic keeps coming back to police mind.

Let's go out through the back door, but don't stop reading.

If you know your mind is a trickster you don't have to hate him or his tricks.

Or your dreams.

I'm against time.

Contretemps habitual is an unintended ritual.

Lies, birds, words are the travelers in neutral gender.

Logophilia comes to mind as Billy the Kid comes to town.

Walk me through the flame, and don't stop talking.

Poetry's self-argument doesn't argue back.

The shoot-'em-up quality of desire's spoken out loud where it happens.

Time teaches beyond our tricks.

No substitute for a life line.

Religious doubletalk delimits no fun intended.

Nothing is ready for prime line.

Truth spoken shames.

More licks than pricks.

Go slow to let intense time line take hold and not kill you.

Dangerous laughter starts solitary.

No status of a statement is just telling.
There are more ways to say your name than Shakespeare spelled his own.
The way birds arrive on a wire a poem attracts meanings to the hardwired heart.

Apparent distraction dictation dictates its subtext.
If you think you chose your poetics please lie down on the couch: how'd it all begin?
If you can, you can and they can put it in a can.

Can't help stepping in the differencing shadow of my unexperienced life.
Who reads with a sense of textual equality on a model of say racial equality?
If the text is a trap at least it shows a thinking traps.
Drums teach words how to be all along.

I'm not who speaks in mind but choose who to be today.
I play with sticks more licks than kicks.
I only truly love music I've never heard.

No words are born to get along.
Poetics is the mindfulness of poetry, so take a real good look.
Friends talk about themselves in their sleep.

The book arises as the line which is always only line by line.
Web dignity is laughing to smithereens.

Facts are never as sure of themselves as they make out.

Poetry takes your meaning away to freshen it free of tyranny.
Now mind leaves you on this side of thinking the other side.
Fair is fair is fair if I may borrow a racket.

Syntax lays back to retain without refraining.
Can't find my truth brush retains an accent.
It's like saying we're guarding truth and shame on you despite the rush.

Meaning retention demeans all hidden intention equally.
Talking funny is a language unto itself.
Expect less than nothing.

What kind of poetry embraces daily even briefly to know all through?
The time for answering questions has passed.
Writing is eating to live.

Somewhere along the line I forget how to be sentimental.
The poem reminds me when I need the torsion.
Even as I write I look at the time, sigh full body.

Frisson frees.
The question passes up time once it crosses the lip-brain barrier.
I can't see the faces of the thoughts throwing the rocks, so dark the time.

Lying reveals the reflexive mode of language in the ascendant.
A poem is the site of self-trickery.

It's my meat that hungers says Hermes in his role as inner wild child.
Transition is what happens when your foot crosses the limen as you catch yourself.
Slogans are never slow enough for poetic justice.

Instant response tells instant truth.
Deliberation qualifies by deliberate quality.
Differending has no ending and no mending.

Now that we spoke loosely can we seek out the cracks for self-deception revelatory?
Some dark thoughts have had their eons and are free to go now.
History is too ill behaved to be believed.

Self-importance is a tight grip.
I apologize to my coffee for missing her creamy swirl, mother of dragons.
Mythic time or real time incalculable dreams us in windows looking out.

Who can say what thorns I skirted to get here and still feel nowhere?
Is the reader my partner escaping or my jailor refining?
Marking time is fondling fiction.

Tricksters hide tracks but I hide nothing as telling does it all.

In dreams engines return abilities
Ontononymous the Particular

Histories talk haltingly, like dreams don't end they go home.
Too much money is rephrasing.
And dreams talk too much, a syntactic call to arms, lips.

The cloud and I see eye to eye.
In the lingual wild word orders quicksand.

I reverie a distant too young to mother mother teaching a poetics of miracularity.
She gives birth to freshly unpreparing the mind.
Or it's only a dream erasing scream yet the Turkish rug sees you seeing.

Alternatively art lives literally.
Trip over a stone knowing is teaching me trust.
Poetry is the bottom falling out from above, as high as you get.

Lies are the parts of the truth useful in blocking the unwelcomed.
Consensus has practical value and mental hazard, as dowsers doubtless confirm.
Playing stops playing upon deciding.

We haven't advanced one bit.
Beauty's unthought.
Oneiric gates leave you standing out.

No one believes when you say what you mean.
The syntax traps the gate open.

every sound its word

Leave out this line and you leave out life itself;
all is chaos again.

WILLIAM BLAKE

Begin poem! begins the poem when you can only write what you write.
One idiolect after another line after line talking their way through.
I can only write a life whatever the obsessing subject.

Declaringly my life has always been perfect that no other version serves the same.
A hard text weaves its way through my soft spots.

You can never make peace with contraries leaves meaning saved in the nick.
A man poet is who calls *she* pulling happiness from the cracks.
No stopping the world giving birth to itself her self's saying.

Thinking's any possible thought moving on.
Getting situated as if veiled has its way with words.
Agenda goes gender neutral except she's still felt as I act.

In the undréamt wild of language word orders quicksand.
I saw it written on the wall that made me think writing on the wall.
On the big page you read whole bodied and time experiences what's never felt.

Any pain teaches its elusive release self secret.
Being really in my body makes me wonder who's really in the language.
A word feels pain saying it.

The truer it feels the newer it wills.
It says *me* saying *it* because I work here too.
It can't be said enough ways to be said wholly.

A self true fool has no choice but to persist in folly.

Not I, not I, nor the mode that blows through me.
Mystery is that a swirl is always *this* swirl.

The unit is not the line it's the mind in play here.

Can't think what I now think means I might be thinking for real.
The newer it feels the truer it wills.
Leaving *should* at home's a must.

The sequence thought is telling therefore the great interest and futility.
Truth spoken shames to be.
A line rides on the same to change in appearance.

I forgot the line, eternity escaped.
Demonstrably monstrous cracking open remembers.
Garuda egg awareness it thinks me that.

People cage and hate cages at once.
A poem, a cabin, a hideout, holding in, hidden hut, homeless break.
It's hard to find a place in this house to lie down.

Eternity the escape artist itself traps in remembering.
I'm skeptical of my skepticism that it hide believing it formulates truth.
The unit's not the line felt now but the mind that gets the girl, code for swirl.

I see the size of the unfound words, the number, the smell, the feel, but not meaning.
Self redeems in the writing unknowing and the natural otherwise.
Poem stops when you begin to write what you should, *danger!*

So you never heard of the dragon dakini.
Clearly your myth is holding back.

Don't think you know what I'm doing, she said, if *I* knew I'd tell you. Straight.
Straight enough for me, I said, makes my tongue curl.

The modality sans modus comes to mind.
She says dance and I dance.

The quality of earliest morning is feeling talked to through, working here now.
On what I'm working on now means I am now on working on now. On's timely.

Now you understand how I understand.
Mind makes shells before garudas.

When she talks funny an egg is cracking.
To say it true is to hear it true.

Bad birds fly higher to escape the shell, show and do.
Break on through. This is for you. So you know.

And it's only the upper edge.
Scratch across the paper, leave tracks, poem trails, leading ledge.
Mind swirls, see inside.

Arbitrarily I'm obsessed with her, the moving and swerving in.
The will is the pleasure in erasure per verse.
It hears in the measure as you go and shows through.

May every sound be its word. There, said.
Language is weighing at your mouth's expense.
Timing is the business of reading.

A thing is said to complete a world without end.
Biblical proportion's living distortions.
To think its way sees a world in symbol.

Half here before it's here, you take the rest and go forth.

Word power backs forward.
Can't say I do force.

Desire scales to the occasion yet its force to mean is scale invariable.
Finger marks. No point pointing.

Puzzling you'll be used up sooner.
Plant talk is fuzzier and logical by haze.
I'm never convinced in a timely fashion.

Why not let things mean their ways?
Conscious words are trying to verb.
Spacing non understanding tumbles to truth before your senses mixed.

Saying how I think thinking is not to make you wary.
Go with the slow is a slogan *in the beginning*.

A poem climbs the stairs in your own two feet.

Time to mumble in symbols, facing.
Self saying says: Respect her to reflect her.
The dangling modifiers keep life sexy.

The poem knows when you're only naked above the eyebrows.
Selves, ssss elves, slaves, lives, loves, never resolve, nor remove themselves.
Lullaby of Birdland sings sexual oology for eggheads.

I other my mind to take it into itself.
I talk dakini to arouse my feminine to the courage of its knowing.
I'm believing in her as my mirrored selfhood believes in me.

Socio whorling wises.
How I finger you imprints and singles you.
Claim every moment empty and see where it gets you, nohow.

Mirroring talks back when you're not looking.
I don't love my image but respect its attachment to me.
I reflect better on you, twice told.

We'll never think our way through this mess.
I have limited appreciation due to the imperfection of the actual path.
Time is a perspective that wouldn't stop even for Jesus.

I'm forgetting how to write which feels weirder than anything.
Last night I dreamt the men who move on and leave us to obliviate.
We're here for the sound being words. Sound being words.

My Business is Circumference
Emily Dickinson

Imagine time forward and time backward as outer bounds of the moving time field.

We're here in the middle, newly aware of having chosen to be here, no there here.

Note the stillness of comprehension falling short at the horizon.

Repeat: We're here for the sound being words where the sound being words.

Two wrong readings make for true, never known before, half known ever.

You can't put meaning together till it puts you back in place, the self-true angle *now*.

"More time is yours—if you want" prophesies my smart phone.

Proving you're on Airplane Mode proves proving finds the law flaw.

Flying is not a place and *nowhere* loses more meaning than it can afford.

Time fields, thought pools.

Verbs are recalled words in flight.

Tongue points in a swirl.

Atemporality or the stillness of the time field operative as a whole is untold.

Mouth, hand, finger, open indexicality, rope dancing, verbals.

An executed word has a silence native to its truth.

And a good book creates its own mistakes.

Zero point resets linguality *radially*, so the arms are opening wider.

Think surround, sense field, feel nothing special till aberrant lift, hold hat, Charlie say.

World is wise before the verb, not to say you or me.

Yet you know it when it sounds like nothing but itself.

I forget what's been written for it no longer needs me.
My vow is to the incomplete.

Speak in exalted tones from salty dog bones.
I promise not to hold the truth from you. Easy. The truth doesn't need me for that.
Poem bites the dust writing what you should and druther not.

Consistency is not a poetic virtue.
Scofflaws sport alternative proving procedures.
Nothing shows up, *surprise!*

In the beginning is the Little Bang.
And Relative & Absolute are never apart.
So she's not mine to start with.

Renaming fames wiser in dark places.
It goes to show the way a dolphin mates multiples.
Darker meaning invisibles register the other radiance.

Gender's zone of vexed identity flexes continuously.
I know me fluctuant.
Models me disorder. That said, come to bed.

Desire is anti-sedimentary.
Subtle startle: *I'm inside the original which is only ever now.*
Take away the line and you take my breath away.

Pronouns are deuces gone wild.

Cruel coercion makes you wait to know, you're born abused.
A title is even less serious about itself than a line.
Poetry holds truth at arm's length down to a pen point pin prick.

Free being centers out, intransitively eviscerating well meaning.
"The most human is only truly visible in the post-human perspective."

A line is an originating vehicle.
Come back it calls to what you're becoming.
It makes no claim to keep up with the finish line.

A poem knows you're only halfway there, no sense pretending.

A thing has the referent it predicts.
"Any being encounters itself through you—how else do you exist?"
I keep being reminded the penmanship is sinking.

Between breaths is the incredible invisible shrinking line.
Feel the gap.
There's accuracy in truly evading.

"I got my site specificity in the bargain basement." Says no one and me.
Poetry is language knowing who it is where it stands.
Even if an angel speaks to you it's a take it or leave it situation.

Crossing out spaces centering.
These are not special effects.
A word spoken true never gives up its silence.

Tip to tap is the alternative map.
A syllable is haptic in the prehensile brain zone.
"I really do mind that you respond direct. You see I'm not the me you see."

Every line is overload.
Naming wild, goddishly given (Hannah) logophrenetics in great outdoor linguality.
You so pleasant me between tongues.

Go tell it on the mountain can also mean no one's listening here below, *attention!*
Slide down your own pole to address the fire that calls you out.
If I reclaimed the seriousness of child's play I could say *Nietzsche!* without flinching.

The word for this day is *amain* as any word that carries its weight—so far, far.
Poetry self-secretly names the mother of language, adoringly.
Here it goes undreaming again.

Reloading as we speak: *Sequencing the rightness of the next closes off.*
Language hides behind meaning, so the fire is invisible.
When it's awake it eludes with color, with tone, with desire.

Anything said has a temperature.
Every sound fills the time it takes to pass you by... the ears.
A meaning has a beat.

Who knew there were so many non-repeating dance steps?
Systems don't catch on in the listening present.
A sound words being outside in.
My hangover is the overhang, lineal loading as we speak.

I started this in the name of the extreme.
Gog knows you live palindromic, the mystery before is the mystery following.
Hannah heals in reverse of expectations.

We're getting there for *she*'s getting there. And why ask for less?
Fortunately this is getting to be a longish life for which no substitute languages so.
Tip your tongue before your hat blows off.

Learning to speak you learn to tweak.
Flying edits. Verb on the fly. Sly mind.
I'm trying hard to soften the sequence but it talks me hand to mouth.

Music at a distance is proof, mind sings awake.
The poem says dance to dance you into life as it is.
This is the wholly registering out of mind. The beat's in overhang.

Tip of the tearing is the top of the mountainous.
I study the mind that tells me to say this.
It's not getting away with everything it thinks.

But I don't understand, I don't understand is the call of the wild.
Getting this far is enfolding further.
The timing is life getting talked into being… this.

Origin is a recurrent recombinant conundrum, dumdidum glossodelia.
It spreads as it's read.
The dangling overhanging a thread, tread lighteningly.
Lightfully is the voice of hers.

Stopping deciding the hand in my hand thinks the unthinkable and squeezes.
Terms of endearment, language embracing from inside the orange, self peals.

Caught up in the drama is the endless longing for endless entrance.
Time to write the message that leaks between letters.
The sentence is pushing back inwards to the unvoiced caesura shaping a door.

What speaks is the impulse, what it means is the pulse.
You know yourself knowing yourself better, now feeling further.
We can't shake the double sense of sense sensing the world having feeling.

Important to disabuse our selves the abused, the used confusing, hope solves not.
We're caught in this net and you sense the strangle holding forth and back.
You can almost get your hands around it and never do. So you sculpt touching.

I notice my walk is self-watching and I almost get my mind around it and never do.
So I touch sculpting. The materia is what comes from everywhere.
Experimental is trying out what is given, most intimate yet zeroed aloft.

Everything is coded but code lacks and sourcing comes up short.
Slacker reading sensation clues.
Walking talking sensory blues—meaning cliffhanger viewing with pulse.

Scholars beware, actual tracks show up in melting snow, and we're watching.
Get my rift?
Lots to close down to get set true and buoy.

Fluctuant gender allows you to render in free fall between us.

If this is still the fall we're listening all the way down.

Like Jerusalem we come and go.
Poetry is a youthful thing and age invariable.
Surrender signs in free-floating pronouns.

Bloodhound nouns.
No dancing with the same feet.
Music is far.

Welcome to where any word finds its pronominal future.
Epic's getting personal and stretching discretion.
I just saw you in my movie or me in yours so doubled is my daily.

Voice is learning to cast itself upon the watery waving.
Signs of the times signing.
It's very personal, says her impersona, completedly convincing.

True poetic breakthrough feels like going insane, scaled syntactic.
Time speeds, but there's hope in dimension, overlays, cross spiraling.
There's beginning middle and end but not in that order and never for long.

The further pronominalization of person(ality) in these talky times is a sign.
Reading the signs is singing the blues.
No time to lose. No *time* to lose. *No time.*

We're adrift in overbeat.
No names need apply.

Hail! is a winter word.
What a line thinks it's saying is beside the point being pointed out.

The dance of *see me/you can't see me* never bores yet makes holes, invisible.
I grow more unthinkful phone by phone.
May every word hear its sound.

There is water which to wade sweeps mind longbodied a world away.
Listening here has a life unknown yet own.
Time is lost by the instant and the syllable.

I thank not my but your stars who have only just arrived.
Hospitality has its own lorn poetics.
Housesitting on the flying carpet puts on airs.

William Blake's at home inside a flare still furthering.
A sentient sentence looks around for new ways out.
Self secret is self inventing and the inferent still to come.

Think this now and never before.

What a line thinks it's saying is beside the point pointing out as we speak.
Incarnation is performative in the very instance it says so. Bow down.
Babel is my babble story back on the lips.

Tongue touching words in a certain sequence equals note struck/mind tunes.
Secret teaching never shows but fleshes the weave.
Begin poem! is spring from down under.

The poem starts before language.

May the forces play fair.

Honor the house here catching mind on the fly.

To think it opens its gates.

Saying listens first in the wild.

Feel the pre-poem pushing up under language.

What is the status of what is to follow is an inappropriate question.

Polish the mirror lest it tarnish thy face.

Not needing to be here yet enjoying every second neighbors a paradise unforetold.

The thematics of presence takes hope for a ride.

"Oops my poem has no subject matter."

Thinking in retrospect is not yet living in retrospect.

A self refining line minimally celebrates deed done, bracing by light embrace.

Firefly flight matches mind flare.

May the tongue twist so lightly words float sense afire.

What I said is how I said it and don't recall.

Still feel the real moving.

Blake didn't say "oops we forgot to have children" but "works are my children."

There's later voice in this reverie at a distance.

My missing personality is very vocal of late.

As you endlessly know we're stranded in the middle of the story, no worry.
Logic resists rhyme until it endures logically.
For example means nothing when consulting the gut.

Put your mind on the line must mean *tip your hand over the edge and onto the ledge.*
Guilt is no love potion.

Waking up in the foreperson is not something you go and do.
Straight to the desert to pray for rain.
Cast your line long to give your fish leeway for wavering appetite.

Truth is only seasonal in a self-organizing sort of way.
Attention spans improbable gulfs in the wild.

Voice strikes a hidden drum in the bodily audium.
A heard word is beyond meaning, even now.
Nothing occludes understanding where nothing is the subject.

Only metaphor with interdimensional leaks need apply.
Rare energy like spring water seeks out every sentient crevice.
You know you're there by the audible glare.

Bad rhyme tells alternative tales *on you.*
Like a zoo on a train you're mated from behind by a stranger unseen.
The thinking now occurring is foreswearing by omission of mission.

I'm contained by cactus and the metaphor of flowering dying.

"If you get the hero itch this is the place to be, sunny side up."
Sadly *The Return of the Impersona* is not yet listed in the schedule.
We're here to surveil the surreal dreams of the real, feet on the sound.

Someone passed the talking fork, time to shut up and eat ear first.
I need tune to tear me loose and float me out.
Please distract my hardnosed insider guards, they're on the take.

If fruit eaten shames, bearing flares fares further.
I hold Eve responsible for the twisting tongue, note signs of Venus mound praying.
No method of transmission is a hundred percent reliable.

When the tongue slips on a word a bird from hell levitates free.
I scare myself sometimes when I let it say me from behind.
There are voices with built in boo.

Ideas play dress-up in my sensorium.
You'd never know this is invitation only.
Time to save on pronouns starting with I.

The self truth that matters has nothing to lose arriving in drag.
A poet's face may map the shortfalls but the tongue retains some serpent power.
Keep trying, keep scrying, and the further exegesis of lying.

No method of transmission is guaranteed enjoyable by a single ecstatic standard.
The proto-civilized interdimensional zoo is ababble at behest of participants.
Peace is a state of consensual non-lethal aggression.
Please hold my hand even if it's under the table.

I get off on my pathetic harmonies in hesitation.
Feeling hard with edge.
Crossing before me she crosses me out.

Note *she* is three words in and three words out and middling in voice I call mine.

I can't help defending myself in the pull to abstraction so I'm going skinny dipping.
Why is the medium so much what wading through falls between fleshy and florid.
Desire is hiding its grammar today.

The substance allows letting the wild beast loose in its own construction.
I can say she meaning licking the soft sides of syllables to ensure dying Romantic.
Holding back harmony adjectival does not hold back harmony verbal.

Grammar and grammaton grasping for glory as against grungy vocals at worship.
It is not just leading us on. It thinks like it rains.
Somatic retains soma as semen retention for the lingual.

I know, the intensity is severe like the weather report in verbal heaven.
She is talking out the side of her verbalium. Genitive neuter, gender fluctuant.
A hot time. Impersona trans grata. Who's hiding where and who's kidding who.

Textual sacrality, scarcity vs. sacristy, schitzy mediation in meditation, I kid you not.
Knowing the page biblically as performative self composure is high posture.
The feet like iambs are on the ground sounds bumping along, so willful.

Freud put penis on the line when he wrote the words *reflexive middle voice*.
Beast self orchestrates in spread leg syntactic straddle.

The eye travels down looking for a high.

The optical tip of the ice wave expands relentless.

There is physics in the matter like poetics in lingualia so let's get it on.

And poetic ecology articulates in having a small carbon mouth print.

Puns comprise reality. In a hurry.

Gossip metastasizes.

Can I write this surface without writing I?

A surface is a body means this surface is this body.

The time is ripe for a pronoun fast.

The self reflexive is the objective self in rebound.

Self reflection is late.

A simple formula goes a long way and a long way from home.

You haven't lived until you've been struck dumb by the force of your own rhetoric.

Life is fly by night.

For time is impossible in the perspective of mind knowing itself.

Words at play comprise reality or vice versa means self acts unbeknownst.

You don't get to take a life off.

Reality is not constitutional to say the least.

Let's say life self organizes and you don't get to know the break points.

But who's counting? is not a fair question.

It counts. And no recounts called for.

Aura is only all around.

One word requires two.
You love words he said but words love me I said so I write down what comes up.
Grammar is the abstraction now possible from singular lingual events today.
The same sentence said by you is now itself.

This moment saying this moment is momentarily more.
I've been hypnotized by her voice.
Walking straight is not an option.

Her *business is circumference* never carries its context far, unless you count this.
The drop off point is the next instant beginning.
Ludwig Wittgenstein means itself as I hear is said.

Twist of tongue is like a lime when the water is cold.
Breath of life, bread the staff, talking stick, strike the rock, linked at last saying itself.
An object has no business proving itself.

Delicious is to the Garden as allure is to linguality.
A fall is through the center or axis yet the pleasure is all mine.
Desire is being called away.

The break point defines the middle.
Her voice lures mood.
Falling off from meaning long beloved freshens the air in here.

My stomach is frowning just like my heart.
I've never been less in control.
It only writes what it does like it rains.

I need help now finding a talking object in the raw.

No dwelling here for long, sad to say.
It's not talking about you, nor even to you. Try through.

Trust is knowing the poem knows best.
Silliness is a phase in unfolding the deadly serious.
Cut off censors at the knees.

We keep looking for a spot in the open that admits not knowing itself.
The poetics of Buddha is non repression in not knowing.
The middle is belly dancing.

Listening harder measures in soft degrees.
The head is not literally on the shoulders for letter by letter it thinks above ground.
My hand is in the water that never passes you by when the ear is partial.

Construe and shoo.
Every action carries away the other it won't be and audibly.
Strange musical fruit is unknowing biblically.

Ear returns to belly and ends up here.
This is destiny where the hero is iffy.
Being soft is not going soft.

Play as you are vs. play to pay.
Reading channels the text.
Text in the raw turns out not to be the object aforementioned.

The hope to get it done before you die puts it on the spot like a leopard in snow.
Helpless beauty doesn't mean weak.
You have to sweep far and wide to let every gesture feel like itself.

Some words are strippers.
Literary speaks to the department of mind enjoyment, so we let it in sparingly.
No need to flee to see to be or be free. (*refrain*) "You're getting sleepy" (*her voice*)

Some thoughts can't get through less trippingly.
They put us on notice to notice, lest we go into free fall between letters.
Becoming lettered has a literal dimension.

The proto-tattoo telling stays told at surface.
We're reminded that nature never sleeps, not really.
Physical flashes of insight hit mind hard, and it's never not rebalancing.

The really interesting absurd is deadly serious right through.
Nature never expects to be read correctly from the start, so why should the line?
It rains the way it speaks, and that goes both ways.

Language secretly desires to never say the same thing.
Part of me wishes to say not really after anything said. Or right in the middle.
Tongue lashing is nature in its mode of operation and reflexive.

The pronominal gap opens wide.
Not making sense feels like failure but it's more like exile starting now.
I'd know her voice regardless.
Grounding finds yourself at zero.

Naming is magic good or bad or how else did you get yours?
This is a near dream explanation.
History is a variable invention making herstory inevitable.

This is a self-waking nightmare.
The Buddha you see before you is in withdrawal.
Meaning is in what it does to the mind.

Hortus conclusus, enclosing enclosure springs out of nowhere.
This is not news in time.
Hyphens over determine and rhyme timely with hymen.
Life shifts levels without notice.

Truth teller's paradox says I never fully tell the truth.
This is a stream under which a stream runs the other way and under that crossing.

A zero minus game prevents us from giving up direct contact with our own zero.
The uncertainty principle applies to emotional tone, feeling it changes it.
The word you see alters before it reaches you.

Verbal personality is an extra in our cast, we keep it under contract.
The motto is *hold further what you behold*.
Any order of language intimates in the interanimate context holding close.

World changes by the page.
The time line heads down reaching toward high.

Self true making is inexcusable in a god's eye.

The voice of poetry is inappropriate.
Content doesn't stay in the head, hence the need for concrete extrusion.
The thought of origin is shifting its locus as we speak.

The page is a spill site.
Poetry cleans up post-tribal mess with a post-namable order of quote chaos.
Clear seeing lets anything seen loosen its grip.

Proud thinking can't resist thinking it knows truth.
The lure to philosophy forces a rejection.

A title throws an object into the textual pond like the genius loci's libation bowl.

Origin is a convenient focus in service of this moment between us.
Forgive me for getting personal but I'm having trouble finding my impersona.
She's pulling the strings nevertheless.

"It's time to stop pretending you've only been pretending."
Zero point is in a romance with storyline.
Intimacy reinvents grammar.

The strangest places are learning to speak in their half breed tongue.
The line is just a sidewalk and the page a neighborhood.
Days are the short form of a short life.

The fall is apperceptual and bad for the neighborhood.
You have to believe in where you stand long enough to let the mad voice speak.
Now the word plays through at variance with itself to find what it has to say now.

Thinking the truth of a line gazes into your image in the pond.

Poem in itself pushes the conclusion that interpretation is a cheap thrill.
This thought is likewise thrilling ass backwards.

If the page narrows I get claustrophobic like my brother's pillow smothering me.
When it gets personal I feel the marketplace is nigh.

There are sixty-four rhetorics in a deck of cards hungry to tell your fortune.
Art has a cost that can't be expressed in price.

Secret signs exist to remind the undecidable everywhere is sustainable.

Reading real is making meaning instantly no looking back.
I'm only half conscious here and that half is half falling on its face.
How many haves make a hole?

Thinking I know it is thinking it's me.

Referential mania bathes in the cold light of concretely expressing stars.
Still there's a refusenik in the heart of every bright thought.
Poetry has long loved agony, hence the impossible language for impossible things.

Primordially the wish is take me at my word.
Still planning on the pronoun fast for slimming down in egoland.
The desire for a stable center swaps out for a centering swirl.

Poetry is training for the great escape reshape.

What you know shows.
It never says what it means.

I picked up the orange juice with full-glass conception and it flew to spill.
Mind congratulates itself laughing.
Autoludoerotic behavior is selectively blinding.

Imagine this line as distributed downward paging to a possible end.
Whole of an ancient evil, I sleep sound. [A. E. Housman]
Quoting climaxes before you.

Slim down the objection.
Sex the healer is banished in our town, O sing.
Completeness does not preclude degrees of self sensing.

Can you see the strutting and fretting in your particulars before light dimming?

Great tragedy jokes with a straight face.
When I know you better I'll show my literary wounds.
Blindness is a matter of degree with salutary thresholds.

Escapism heals sequestering invisible help.
Now you see me now you don't.
Ecstasy is the other option hiding from view.

Slim down erection. Give up inspection.
In the wholer contact no walls no flails.
Language makes every effort to divine truth enwinding.

You've spent your life explaining how you are and why, take a break.
Time to stop stopping timing.
You can dance to it and not lose the stance in it.

Attention heats.
Sex extemporates.
New to the few includes you here now.

Disappearing slogans ink only the air.

Please find no hidden meaning trees rejoicing or not.
Language keeps saying it's making every effort to divine its truth in saying.
Take it at its heard.

I no longer recognize my own desire, said looking her in the eye.

My elemental earth extruded apparel is flashing in my mirrors, your eyes, my ears.
Life the flyby has me enjoying the view.
I'm dreaming my elements into a body to come. Stay tuned.

Sex temporates when you take your temperature in full flagrante without agenda.

If you can do it in linguality you can be done with and by it here and now.
It may be time to trap the wild metaphysicality that hiccups our best ideas.
When you know it's so it shows.

What season is it today?
Secret teachers never show except through.

I write nostalgically under the sign of the four. Now back to zero.
I tell you authorship is the damnedest thing and nautical.
My inner personae may join facing outward in consensual surround.
Poetry teaches me I'm an experimental person.

Alternate destinies appear to gather at the horizon.
My inner beings have been circling the wagons again.

Metastatic gossip may be reaching unto trees.
Primary therapeutics teaches writing on air.
Poem harvests running insight regardless of creed or diagnosis.

Between knowing(s) caught in unreadable script and scripting are catching.
Ancient teaching still laces with tongue action filmic.
Resist metaphoric consistency lest it hook you between readings.

The hermenaut's request spaces the forces pushing from the other side.
Traumatophilia motivates the bolder inner johnny appleseeds.
Biodiversity takes root psychodynamically embracing alien ways.

I can't think these things without prosthetic pathetics.
The uncertainty principle is nature protecting herself against phallic mind.
I embrace the irreducibly other and subvert gendering historics.

On the other hand I am not the authority on this page.

If there are gods on this planet bird feathers big beaks songs signing are their play.
Sexual haptics heals the wounds of desire so there's a poetics to come.

the eros of soft exterior shocks

for Robert Kelly
embracing his 80th

I'm thinking metaphors in my sleep like conversations with dead philosophers.
Here we are again in the moving center.
Friend is never far between.

The poem is its poetics when over time its consequences are inescapable.
Only the reader holding in will ever know.
Verbals stand in relation.

Our misunderstanding is mutual.
It holds together as we speak.

There's more entry prize in walking naked sacred.
Text sources the unperceived by way of the underread.
No surprise there. Nor running scared weird.

Verbals sit recovering.
It holds together as I speak, as if talking to myself, but I'm not all here.
Our misunderstanding is intimate.

Oscillatory focus is open in the middle and sharp at the edges.
I river to keep my banks apart.

Thinking metaphor is knowing between things, drawing from secret slush funds.
No comparison. Just sounds.
Reference is mask.

Shifting weight, lifting clouds, behaving days.
A complete statement is true in itself.

Time is what can put you in a panic for no good reason.
Having a body my line is commanded from the inside.
Digestion never ends.

One day the earth will digest me.

Environment is my side inside out.
It depends the whiches it says I say. Day by day.
I never told you otherwise nor not either.

I wear my house and I don't go out.
Mute trancelike concentration is drumming on itself in my temples.
Co-perception has a technical base and a spooky outcome.

Blood syntax has thinking pulse.
You'd know her voice anywhere.
She'd rather be awkward to be right, the co-perceptive line of sight.

So what's my line?
And what's mine about it?
It *sets life cutting into life*.

Knowingly sexual healing is bottom up in the wild.
Not all freed modifiers can be said to dangle in plain sight.
Seeing thus poetry digests but is not necessarily itself digestible.

I forgive you for my misunderstanding since error is mutual.
Symmetry is nightmare and no face to face.

Days self-disrupt without notice.
Life teaches the practice of its timing.
Therefore no therefore.

A text can be that never fully reads all the way out.
A poem is language with undertow.
The fact that almost anything can be said about it is tellingly what it is.

All modifiers dependently originate in thing thinking, even.
Guests in my worn house are invited to continue speaking silently.
We're hearing wherever however.

Now is that I can only read what you are reading here inside.
Time is another matter.
The poem makes enzymes for transmigratory bird wording.

Actual length being non-convenient the mind turns outside time.

Writing can be further conditioned just as orgasm's not personal.
Every statement is out of context once spoken.
Matter is timely.

The text proposes the future now fact non-accomplishing.
Look up writing down.

Simurghs are nontransmigratory bird wording to free mind zones.
Shall we go?
Problematic is getting a wing up.

Enter from around the side, please.

It's late, have I done enough to merit going free range on the blank life page?
Mystery is dime a dozen frozen but once lingual *in the flesh it is immortal.*
And rimes with portal so come with me.

Staking a claim ends up sexual in the state of nature.

No more bellicose historical erections sticks good on the bumper.
Orgasm is not autobiographical.
Shifting freight, lifting attitudes, displacing platitudes.

Language is playing with me again.
I suffer from post-noncomprehension stress syndrome.
Is the nautilus mollusk happier knowing it lives inside the golden mean or are we?

Yet knowing is not a clear concept and in a timely sense not a concept at all.

Every piece of my puzzled assortment finds its place in its own time.
Ex post facto coming out of being after the fact of fact itself is retro and spectacular.

Is the markhor goat holier than thou knowing it butts with the golden mean?
The wall it hits is neither harder nor softer than heaven's gate.
I'm not saying I know this. Mine in season by riming reason.

For I wear my golden mean meaning on the back of my mind.
It's a load like love. Hard word.
It calls itself into question so you don't have to: use freely.

getting labile in the lab

Wisely and slowly they stumble who run East.
fortune cookie at Ho's Szechwan Restaurant, Altadena, 1972

I dreamt the world is asking us to be in it and discovered I wasn't asleep.
And so I invented story whose nature is to do in us on the inside of the world.
I had to be right but the fire was too hot.

The poem is juggling times the more the merrier.
Intoning inner voices from beyond is more like earth rumbling than spirit whistle.
It gets wordy like rip tides and can take you out to sea in a sieve.

Never too many likes.
Likes are truest like a waterfall. Think rainforest and high cliffs.
And mumbo jumbo suddenly attaining vine-inspired clarity.

Heartbeat is not as regular as it sounds. Sounds. Sounds.
This could go on forever in a timeless non-moment, no momentum, still point.
There's no point and no promise of a point. I'm on my own out here over here.

We have taken a turn for the verse.
Statements of course speak for themselves.
We don't so much use language as intermingle with it.

Authorship is putative.
Poetry would love happy endings if it didn't love happy middles more.
It's on vacation by force of its power to vacate.

Rhythm is time relocating.
Thought-provoking putativity sounds just like labile reflexivity.
The boat is rocking itself.

How many no's can balance on a gnoeme?
And then there were gnoes even as there were not…

Creaturely emergence is hunting down strange foods.
Sounding *down* cuts the path.
Obstruction by baubles slows bringing brilliance into regulation.

It's its own language which to speak is the one-way tube to transnativity.
Home estranges biodiversely.
No words are the never before spoken.

No sense looking for the system which finds you knowing.
Grammatical mood: In waiting to see what it wants to be in growing me up.
Evolutionary poetics begins with the poetics of evolution.
We need a name for the units that aren't.

No drama is the never before acted. (*insensate applause*)
No time is unitary but that others cut across.
I'm only happening now is only as true as the reading.

Poetry is language sleeping with its eyes open.
Appropriating the mind voices of others with minimal interference in the élan.

Voyeuring with eyes closed has its secrets disclosed somewhere near.
Heard one at a time before rime *words free*.
Language is alive in that it takes itself back.

---

[1] An evol is an evolutionary entity conscious of its non-binding fate.

Welcome to our town festival of silencing.
Time to tune in at the microfascial underweave of the vehicular tongue.
I read it back to gauge the shout factor on the outskirts.

Lattice mind is waking up to lattice world.

And then there were gnoes even as there were knots...
They take themselves back right before you, no shame.
Time space prestidigitation for whose pleasure is pure speculation. Mirroring.

Identity goes wrong as agency errs.
Out to sea in a sieve images the safety factor in the happiness of the middle voice.
If you can read it you are it.

Lingua is begging me to let her go even as she grabs my ankles at the edge. Safe fall!
It's just a story, get under it.
And no one tells in every mind.

Non-ejaculatory thinking is retentional.
There's safety in zeros.
Axial syntax slipknots its psycho-Babel strands conceptually vacating.

Believe nothing you hear in this house. She lives.
Never slight your whole shebang.

No line fells in every bind.
Nor every breath a poem recovers.
Until does.

We touch heaven laying hands on a human body.
Novalis

Nothing is real now but it retains in tongue.
Blind self-certainty is different for the seeing and the blind.
I'm only a poet for never being born one.

End of story and starting here.
Breathing grieves its unbreath to guide her home, hands down.

Language is the spread factor in the transmission field.
Poem is the matter emerging before it knows what it is.
The sense of self here is the way Italians talk with their hands on the phone.

There's a poetics of don't ask just do and what's to say?
I'll go further: I'm used by language.
Spores feed on us till we eat through to other further.

Poem is always already happening and then you know it.
The primal site is now or never.

Life doing signals all future life and lives.

It takes no effort to complete.
As long as it speaks she *is* unidentifiably.
I regender further the further I go.

Poem reading is where life makes itself up through you.
The panic of completion forgets completion.
You can't know further but further and further.

To me the guitar represents my music that's inside me, but external,
you know what I mean?
So I guess that's why it's like having a dick. It's like, myself, but out.
                                                        Amy Winehouse

You know in your blood the work you do runs through you.
Bird makes nest is duty.
Every moment its own last moment.

I awoke today wondering how to fit the infinite inside the finite without cracking up.

I read my work to relearn its language while not getting stuck with its story.
Otherwise our intimacy would be elsewhere.
I find myself now or never.

A house shape-shifts until it knows what it is.
Your room has insight and enough to spare to share.
My body is always trying to be its first nest.

Ancient in building means sounding intelligence from the ground up.

For any absence of a subject-verb assume a suppressed pronoun has slipped back in.
Living lines are never arbitrary and always contrary, inside outside all the way.
The intimacy of cross-purposing is a secret.

True marriage were two people two sides of the one coin spending.

Pronominal tests are everywhere, no?
When the line gets me I know why I was born.
Then *poof!* free again from knowing.

Sherlock Holmes is more real than a lot of people I know.
Susan Quasha

Great lines must take care not to choke on themselves.

This feels like a newscast from the (re)birth canal, pushing, pushing through.
And we're out!
This heaviness must be signals from the part of me still dragging behind.

We live by two calendars, one withheld from conscious embrace.
The bird's egg knows moon rules the body intimate.
This feels like one foot's wet.

The crazed wise angel saves me from the sleep of wisdom.
Meanwhile life lumbers to the finish like a bankrupt contractor.
Wake up it's late. (*I'm still talking to myself*)

I'm sensing by dermal linguality.
Touch me here I feel you there.

I catch myself dreaming of forceful surrender and I shake sleep loose.
It's coming down to zero unit of human.
Read me here I'm there aware.

A little bird is saying *already lived that up*.

Is heaven so limited in capacity that there's only room for the good?
Read me there I'm nowhere.

I can't seem to stop doing breath thinking.

Skin is our internet, and now I can say *she* and mean more by far.
I admit this feels itself worshipping without recourse to such *word*.
Shaking out language from suspects in hiding I detect then weave back through.

Anything said projects a terrain.
I'm closing in on reflects in habiting. Inhabit the cracks.
Text has this texture as in holding in hand and hand.

The closer is emptying, and emptier is closer.
I can't stop holding her hand, I'm holding fast in attachments adoring.
Otherwise I would never know that it starts empty.

I stare into the eyes of the time at hand letter by letter.
Spell casts graphologically, spelling casts and creeps the page crossing.
Grammar shamanism has to hide its intimacy.

Centrality is instant specific and space mobile.
First mark is genie release.
Hence the dangerous impact on neighborhood is topically applied.

Every effort to help pushes further away.
Lingual prison break precedes further capture.
I put pen to paper to draw blood.

At last I'm touching Lorca and his hiding under page duende.
A stroke of the pen signals death—the dance is on.
The page is the blank with ears.

I'm timing my slide to catch the view.

The more you touch the more I say you.
I have to score this ambienting noise to feel the pulse handily.

A voice teaches its listener how it means.
The words caught up go indirect to swipe a curve new.
Life is dimly asking to crawl out from under prevailing knowledge blankets.

The touch is coming into being.
To be ready to say the thing must first become unsubstantial.
There's a tongue trick the trip up the upper lip rides through to call me out.

We don't know how we got here.
The best speculation is like it says a mirror reflecting further.
This is relationship, ship with sides on sides over water, wave sound standing.

Wisdom is a wise woman undergoing old before forgetting young.
Mind is self-honing.
Provisional ontologies flare and fluoresce against the dark.

Mind points but also swoops its latent goods.
A lost poem is death before its time.
I thought *being is happy in its nature* when the spider took my thought away.

A poem is a death risk on purpose.
The aim is better not understanding.
The art is being in and out of your skin knowing time's up from the start.

Time speeds by and I am a rider.
I hit my head against the page and it won't let me in.
Suddenly I'm feeling myself the object of a lucid dream.

Letting out some joyful shouts too long cooped up in here.
We're still in the time of cutting down on pronouns.
Name to body is title to poem and ever the twain are fleet.

In the last five minutes I slipped into 'toon time further than ever.
Soap opera is the site of our attachment at arm's length, pre-hug.
It feels like Saturday but it's only Friday proves we live in a dollhouse.

I'm at the North Pole stuck, lost, but feel better knowing you'll read this.
I write the date I'm writing to get a penhold in the timing slide of the instant.

Hand writing bad saves the page from idolatry.
The temple is blowing through the sand.

I get writing starting to lose footing anticipating the view on the way down.
Slippage in the truth of time echoes through these pages I date.

Still the undated *first house* is big enough for all lives stumbling on.
Moving pervasive carries the protein of one room to the next.

Movement bonds spaces and then there was house.
Maybe I'm the aforementioned philosopher astray.

I stopped hugging a favorite idea long enough to see clear through.

Beauty is present when not understanding while also not caring.
Eagles overhead!
Now sensing a state neither existence nor non-existence.

Earth's commitment to renewal even cataclysmic erases our alibis.

Life ranges on the outskirts of awakening mind.
Did I say I am?

World resounds with senses I co-own.
Thought made things, and curiously I am feeling thoughtful.
Not only did I not see this coming I can't see it happening.

Verbals in relation make sparks in the dark, when willing.

Thought *things* in the verbal mode further verbing.

The space is an ear and bespeaks its other.
My twoity footholds to the backflow coming.
Reading is reality's dare.

I abuse the page and the blank it protects.
I can't not say the female part is everywhere receiving.

Hwæt!

The discourse of self-true *anything goes* comes on slower than you'd think.
It's the other side of the problematic of political action that one size does not fit all.

Dermal lingualities are all around and I'm a little dizzy.
All modifiers dangle in some measure.
From word to word is around the realm.

Honest-to-god hierograms vanish the instant seen.
No use straining to spy on the unready.
Tissue release teaches more.

Physics induces schizophrenia and poetry enjoins the array.
I cherish every instant of spooky action at a distance.
She's playing dice again behind my back, but turning around all dangles in order.

OK just pretending to be from a contrary dimension and my visa is expiring.
Pronouns flee from modification.
I'd say we were in this together but I'm reluctant to comfort the grammatical.

Sherlock Holmes is outrageously present and curiously *à la mode*.
Imagine him regretting thinking who would not do the same for you.

Reading watches thinking as force without being thinking perforce.
We dangle over the blank.
Daring thinking on the flying trapeze recodes hi res.

Poetry teaches how to talk as not me.
And proving now the dare comes true.

I was nowhere until you saw me.
The sky is signing cumulus on the self-plotting line.

What could it matter that I don't like the number 16?
That question is non-rhetorical and real enough to be unanswerable.

Spicer's little green men live on in the little green words.
Everyone gets tangled in his tangle but only the few hang back in its wilderness.

Quantum weirdness is the particular text simultaneously waving in our minds.
Schizo science is high stakes slack rope walking over turbulent reality cracks.
The riddle that never riddles minds your business you still don't know.

Meaning is back on the fly, the choice is to duck or spread.
I raise my arms as if to praise ET but the secret of this gesture is female embrace.
Clouds part suddenly and sky is undeniable.

Poem as welcome mat attracts all manner of heel, stiletto not least.
Getting through the door *clean* leaves life on the outside and mind still behind.
I ride the mare facing behind to give the future her due.

Expecting the mind to perform like a trained seal is counterpoetic.
A curved spine self-obsesses.
Sequence is not, not really.

The poem was nowhere until you read me.
When matter signals signals matter.
We know each other faster than light, nay, before.

The fall or wave collapse is my definite being, me as you find me and don't.

I'm being watched.

This is not the metaphors I dream, no dead philosophers in arrears *en arrière*.

What can bud does.

Knowing you changes you, and I don't mean who, *what!*

Looking into your eyes I feel faster than light.

Here to there's like children of the sun.

Secretly language can go backwards, timely.

Your gaze shows time spreads, makes room to rise.

Slow down and look around; it's more than a moment abounding.

You can still feel our wilderness yet nothing to see.

I'm at one end and you're at the other and up and down the seesaw lineloops.

If I measure you I stop our non-local flow between.

Poetry reverse engineers birth.

Looking into any swirl invaginates the mind.

Our tongue goes forward to gather back.

When you read me I experience collapse.

Now in many ways I'm feeling at one with the multiverse.

The many worlds interpretation is strictly personal.

I'm being watched from the word, *go!*

If but one lingual surface return upon itself in your ear mind, track switches.

To get ahead of another person you have to get ahead of yourself first.
No god fully figures the order the issue from womb commands.
The self-vaginating mind finds more ways out in a whorl.

The unrealized part flies up from the nest disturbed.
The realized part drops down to core *as if* apple.

There is a judgment allows that denying judging proves judge will be judged.
Justice is unthinkable.

Nothing hurts awake like closing the book on.

The poet dying lays bare the holes in wholeness.
For the force of any statement is how hard it hits in the wits.
Adam ate an apple but eve ate a rose.

What would bud buds.
Self elect true elect.

There are other ones starts with a fact that there's more than one one.
Real art confuses.
Parallel linguaverses or the search for other words.

How, where, and whom it hits, it fits.
Meanwhile reading gets in the way.
There's no time to lose if we're out of time like gas.

Reverse culture to phylogenetic diversity, yeast poetics, be bud again.

Today I got empty enough to feel potential.
Now I'm riding the same till change in the going appearance.

Right timing in lingual time is moving knowingly outside time.
Seeing bundles the world and I diagram its sentence at will, varyingly.

Human life is a set-up.
We're listening for the applause from the upper galleries.
Appearance is how *we* goes to show you.

Time to learn to' read all over.
Ask crazy.
Enter anywhere and meet your daimon. Or die lazedly.

Strong force idea species are as spooky as anything in Blavatsky, but numbers calm.
Immense forces hanging out in minutest environments prove intimacy unthinkable.
And we're still unstable while ever more able.

Anything is possible to believe; there's no not believing; what's true can't not be.
The search for other words is itself the parallel linguaverse long withheld.
Many worlds in my life make *my* more lifelike.

The poet is the last to know the status of her statements.
It's going very far out on your last limb.
Spoken in recognition of these lateral lineal ex—tensions.

Which is to *say retention.*

Keep your eye on the bouncing ball doing the singing.
Fly the coop to keep mind awake or it's a life sentence with musak.
Still here means more than entertained if you please.

It's not hard to tell what needs to keep speaking.
Just tripping does not hear how far the fall.
Eyes open on the way down is a high term of life on earth.

Received lines thin as they go then thread back through newly dimensional.
Pages are planes, plates, plateaus.
Book is block solid with interior flight flow home until fiber turn, and all's still here.

There's temp geometry in glossochemistry.
This sentence is not moving as your eye is or will have been as of *now*.
If you cognize one word or two words at once the sentence blurs; you didn't. Yet.

I'm my own figment.
I'm post-op in and unto the ligaments and their writing ligatures.
On this model poetry is pre-lit and post-hysterical historic.

Keep your figment to yourself does not mean go fuck yourself.

The end is insight in sight.
And the present invention is never without subvention. Undertime.

I mean *she talks to me* is no claim, no shame, no blame, and never to tame.
Literature is talking funny without fear of consequences.
Spoken for only in speaking for as far as the far shore's not so truly far.

Let me be clear syllable by salivating syllable the better to eat you red riding words.
Myth lives in the faerie telling tales on you you live through.
One word at a time leaves plenty of time for crossflow.

Everything you think compromises everything not yet thought.
Still being clearly says it's indestructible.
This saying is untranslatable.

If you think these thoughts persistently they think you.
Time's animal sense animates all.
Meet the director here in the mirror, eh Orphée?

There's a poetry that only begins in replacing a world known.
You have to leave the world to learn it and enter the world new to prove it.

The variability at the end of the funnel is oncoming confusion and panic—stop!
There's a hold at the heart of release still to come.

Getting up steam is summing up strobing frame by frame.
This is thinking on the run.
Everything knowable on this page is roundabout without actually being round.

One word at a time has an inordinate effect on structuring reality like darkening.
There's hope in the thousand and one nights effect of a singular morpheme.
Automaticity passes for synchronicity.

Language corrupts to get clear.
Intransitivity is what gets there for you.

The heavy-mind joke a dying phoenix ejaculates over its egg is truer than it sounds.
Believe everything you read, everything you hear until the world believes in itself.

If there's no right way of reading going back over is the actual beginning.
No back story, only sidewinding rumor mill renewable electric.

Tiny monstrous thing on the table's even now deciding if it's animal or vegetable.
Suspense keeps its kick.

I'm now going to talk not talk.
The sound is ancient beyond Greek mind fleeing the zero.

Dozing midline feeds back through cosmosyntactic cracks.
Approving is proving and proof of disproving, therefore I disapprove.

The book you are reading is not limited like its poet.
Words free to self-limit and no one can stop 'em.

There's a certain relief of thinking in twos like flickering luminous non-duals.
Always listen to sound judgment one octave down.

What does not seduce but alarms with eros turns on otherly.
Don't get wise.

Sing like the bird of paradise at play and away from parliament.
Contemplate connected fruiting bodies for everything aboveground at night is sex.

The lines you follow eyes-open stream mycelia to call a mind to come.

Thinking flees the thinker.
How you say it is how it thinks in you.
No need to get personal.

What is thinkable here is not thinkable there.
Can't locate thought even when I think I can.
Circumlinearity is not so much trackable on this line as self-tracking.

If thought is lightfast it's everywhere at once and no*where*.
Every word has a ledge and an edge as sheer as your nerves.
The linear aspect is at best feel-good.

When Duncan cursed the noisy tech man Taylor Mead said *Get real, Duncan.*
Dragging fact into the present gives it the status of fantasy longing in real time.
Our deep sadness longs for disaster sadly to make common purpose.

From the stars is anywhere outside my range of control.
Secretive nature imitates superpositional thinking when no one's looking.
It doesn't follow. Its logic is alien. Its science is *gai.*

I'm up and down about this coming and going that is life and not. Flickerfilming.
Particulars evade attention by entrancing.
What's true is everywhere in coming to itself.

This may be the work of an ambisinister two left-lobe subgendering impersona.
There's no accounting for.
Thought after thought comes to a standstill yet moves on.

Poetry pretends to be necessary but it's only reality's ruse.
Mind makes whoopee like it or not.
This is the up end of the up and down mooding mind making matter.

Subject got lost last century in the wake chaining grammar to fluid nature.
This is not to say it's literature but it definitely litters.
Life is upset that earth is pissed.

O dream on and don't stop for a cognitive snack.
Bounty first and no need to count.
I dislodge and think dawn.

There's no need for these threes.
Their lovelife's smack dab in the middle.
It's got two ends and is all beginnings.

I take *watch your step* literally.
And toe the line.
Letters link time tale and sexual talk.

Feel the inward wet and warming in the *X*ing swirl?
It's the secret meaning of syntax cracks and crackle.
Linguality strives toward the unconditional.

Ungendering proves the lure is real, so I say *her* to *say* her.
Ponder. Lay her egg. Hold her tongue. Hear her hind sight looking up.
Words are birds when they wing away new.
There is life after language in the lingual afterlife.

At root you own all sound.
Anything ever historicizes the tongue.
I'm a nay-playing gender distending eleusinian aspirant judging by the breath.

Two negatives, three, you name it makes a positive capable of fluctuant pro flow.
Self-negation flourishes in its own aftermath.
To read in neither-this-nor-that mode is not refusing to choose.
Towers are unworkable as talking sticks.

Fixation constricts, let's face it, Janus.
On this logic the rain forest is a zoo on the grand scale.
And this is the logic that does not follow itself.

The line lives always a milliverbal ahead of knowing where you are and how.

There's an owl inside howl all about laurel-degradable repeatable prose poesis.
Things are going trippingly by the feel of falling.
Machine mind now knows how to read your moves before you decide to make 'em.

It trips you up to know what's making before you make.
Where's the heartfelt foretell freed from control greed?
Person pretense is less and less baiting breathable. No can say.

No can tell. No is subject to your verb. To heart.
No is not against nothing. No requires continuous adjustment not being logical.
Its danglers are life lineal.

My heart finding the spot on the porch or on the page releases the thought.
Like lightning no allegory, no alibi.

Poetic effect includes thinking in circles so we break out.
Lingual measles call for escaping the prisonhouse of linguality addiction.
I'm not making this up.

All arguments are circular on the energy plane.
The feet grip like god's bite and there was metric.
Monitor the flow blow by blow and it gets to be a show.

Show yourself.
The burning bush provides no cover.

No noumenal naming in the word shed.
The double film layer on the just creamed coffee is soulful ghostly.

Living layers. Clustering empties.
Welcome to the post-bottled world.

Any fixation constricts as any friction conducts.
And no lack of contact in the tongue.
It slows to heat more trippingly.

Folding money, personal values, thinking light, fruiting bodies.
Nobody knows the trouble I've seen.

Negotiate tongues like a mountain path with steep cliffs.

As we know by now language is still learning how to mean.

The daimon of the moment knows itself in what you say.
Selves, sssss elves, slaves, lives, loves never resolve.
Close-up phonemenolgical unfolding saying effectively disrupts prevailing views.

Life lines hand you your personish pen writing ripening stripes.
That thought fails to establish a mode of critical reception.
It wasn't thinking in the way expected by the question *What were you thinking?*

I've lost my train as in training wheels and dog gone.
Language is always hiding something like burying its bones for another day.
The inner animal is not behaving today.

Do you believe in the hereover?

Marriage is finding your double heart and never knowing till now quite how.
The work is avoiding critical deception.
Textual texture draws life out of hiding in the mind.

Just think, *now.* Over easy, speaking squeezy.
"Love is like talking to yourself in an unknown voice."
Stayner it said from the sleeping world by my lips. Stain her? No way. Stay near?

At 3 AM I also dreamt the organ of apocalypse.
All the while it's showing me its self-sensible language gift.
This *mens mentis* only feels like a rift *absconditus.* Now!

The Ego's dead, long live the Ego!
Perspective by history and by reverie are equally reliable life guides darkly.
Most fun is watching your own chess game as both sides playing against the middle.

Language includes non-language or you wouldn't be able to speak at all.
Only what is also not itself can say nothing properly.
Just think about who you're not being when you're most yourself, say hello.
She's starting to feel like this is home.

Self-sculpting entities do excitatory transformation of the incoming signals.
The only reliable map is the one you are making while lost.
Mountain paths with steep cliffs step by syntactic step.

Go barefoot to evolve.
The poetics switches opportunistically.
Poetic fundamentals do not spread their legs for fundamentalists.

Who'd'uv guessed syllables feed back originary charge?
Gynophorics, for example, the transportive force of fruiting bodies.
Physical beauty bearing her enemy built in still calls us to hold her outside in.

Any one thing's nature's mind door found feeling along in the dark sensing danger.
Why think a known thought when you can look into her lap of earth being first?
You still know the dragon when you see her eye to eye.

Déja entendu is the literal divining line by line.
Again reading is the same unknown new.
And now receiving permission to enjoy this moment—just in time!

I'm still hollowing out the present instant to make my cave vaster.
I seek the vistas of one who rages in his cage.

Everyday the poem rite invents me new but not my shoes.

How do you mean? I ask myself now otherly.
Any given line may dream a rabbit punch to the back of ideology.

My hand is behind my back with a hollow grip on potential.
This can only be said when the mouth is overfull and desire raves on.
It catches the line before she lays on air with our lustful curve.

Now don't go tracking my sounds to mean the more you need, she cautions.
These sounds leave no tracks but lacks.
There are still lessons to unlearn.

Tripping on stones I half recall the ritual lithics that aroused my mobile self sense.
Self-sacrifice is unknowing.
Compassion is self-interest at the level of page and turning between.

Life does not keep its appointments.
You won't get far without your lasso.
I dog these metaphorics as allegorics lest they fail to logodegrade.

Being on the right side is not good enough in these rugged peaks and vales.
Hyper-emphatics is bad feng shui.
The middle way implies a hole as big as your house.

The body of writing calls up grounded radiance only.
This accords to sotto voce universe subtalk voicing what you can't know yet sense.
The claim is forcefully prepersonal where pre suggests an ecstatic near.

To die for metaphorically means to live for while never not continuously dying.
If you step in this river twice it's now the same as never before.

I say to myself avoid getting stuck in the tale you're pretending to tell.
Not all lines survive till the periodic thresholds nor minds.
The poem wants the reader to become what it is only now becoming.

I am the first reader and in this critical phase treat the page as a crime scene.
Birth closes indefinite mind including demise.
Caught in the folding unknowing I glimpse being of this planet.

I don't experience the gap calling this up but only the tug into flow.
First signs of lava mind.
Never forget the hearth beckons with originating fire.

Infinite regresses in the re-enfolding field of self-foregrounded rejointing lines.
Some things are only unsayable when the mouth is fully open.
The fire that cooks itself remains raw.

Deeper and deeper the self-unsaying is our nursery rhyme.
Dulling the senses makes the heart go wild.
The sex is a holder.

The fantasist of mouth-foaming for freckled flesh is not personal here.

Never to have had this thought exactly as it is is poetic starting now. Now.
On the other hand there is no this, it's too quick to be itself, moving on then.
The feel is the only thing real enough to call itself thing, still feeling it.

Now then is how mind turns shaky knowing into thoughtful sequence.
But does it work? Does it do any work? Or is it a freeloader biblically speaking?
Beware of what sits around doing nothing but stealing Mom's money.

I say *Faith!* It promotes the possibility the cord will open the parachute.
This means riding the space of intention still undisclosed, but I hear something.

The poem can be humming inanities *I get my lovin' in the ev'nin' time,* unlistening.
Meanwhile the poet is courting the dawn behind her back.
Time to bring sacred hypocrisy out of the closet.

The full stomach makes room suddenly at the mention of dessert. Fact.
The full life finds space for human interruption. Fictive certainty.

Poetry avoids seduction by sounding minute frictive alarms.
Shocking indicates a sudden transfer of current.
Personality numbs.

Eye friction ignites.

I'm always still wanting her back while looking her in the eyes.
I know what I know stepping off the track.
I hide my last judgment in every word spent.

What my work doesn't have is everything it has.
Unresolvable questions seem obsessed with my mind.
They know what I don't know, how scarcely mine it is.

Every instant faces the need to reconcile inside with outside but it never lasts.

Forgive the thinking that is happening in the line as key to forgiving your own.
A line has a light leading to its end beyond the flash.
Writing is looking at itself in the mirror in your *hand*.

Believing the world begins in this instant is almost impossible, however vital.

Rhythm includes dilation.
A shock creates its own space and mind pools.
I'm practicing to be the servant of this moment, asking, and you are helping me.

New Year's resolution or epitaph: *to be in eternity as I speak.*
The text questions by not answering.

I can't grasp not being here.
I'm mourning lost language and strategizing to get it back.
Grief cannot resist disbelief.

You cannot grasp impermanence.
It hurts to lift a lantern in disbelief seeing the way through syntactic strangeness.
Looking for an honest pace.

If I tire of my words I tire of my life.

We are the species that tells itself stories to make it all okay.
It *is* okay but we doubt it, need to explain, *yakety yak don't talk back.*
Like the empty with its hidden fullness the unsaying says the more.

To say it has a mind of its own is as accurate as *own* expressed can be.
Religion is sacred jury-rigging; it teaches jury-praying.
I hide my last judgment in every word spent freely.

Words are not always words but wetlandish source sites.
The now of variable life is all my hopes and fears and release into many and none.
All here all the time goes for all and any alls.

The thoughts I think often come as first in their thinking.
No more pretending to own: *thought is to the mind as light is to the eye.*
As truth is to "my" reality, so the stranger than fiction attractor gets "me".

Threes are intrinsically asymmetrical as I dream Dante knowing.
Beatrice is trouble where it hurts gloriously.

She exiles me in my very singularity and the marriage of true ones.

Gap, gape, what comes apart takes apart.
What comes in its order takes heart in the missing part.
The my-ness of the world is gathering intelligence with all things intelligential.

Last night I realized I'm not a person but a station.
Microsensing wetland verbacules are hiding selves between stations in the way.

You can't be expected to know when you've been brought in behind the scenes.
Momentary balance is fundamental human gesture given inevitable falling forward.
Discriminating surfaces no way attitudinizes in effect.

Nobody knows but Jesus no longer makes it to the lips.
Baptism never ends for her naked beauty rising up from Allapattah water even now.
Seeing from the end is being the light at the end of the tunnel.

The field is occupying mind.
We stood up human over rocky terrain shoeless flatless bare.

If my sensate free mind zone attracts self-strange entities how can I object?
Counting blessings is painting birth defects by numbers.
I don't intend meaning but inhabit meaning-hungry matrices.

Any devil who speaks to you is a devil worth speaking to, said Mr. Kelly as lifeguard.
Progress is deepening the present occupation instantly.
Sly truth slips in as a sidewinder.

I've thrown my figurative arms around some ghoulish contraparts.
They soon scatter loved.
Eyes closed to the harsh avoids no marsh [Fortune Cookie from Hell]

We're not at the crossroads we are the crossroads.
I apologize to the goddess for my cruel self-dismissal.
A moment let all the way in lives all out eternity.

Between us the text is the secret endlessly for this instant only.

sound talk

for Benjamin Boretz

Time to enjoy the neverbefore said.
I'm here to tell you I'm not telling you.
It sounds like I'm making it up but my senses tell me it's making me up.

The line wanting to be the greatest ever outlaws itself in the nick of time.
Desire is lawless.

The middle of any phrase or phase is free from its consequences.
Mind has secrets like its float zone.
Timing is voluntary. And then it's not.

Instantly along the way sound frees knowing nothing.
Music teaches how not to decide right from wrong.
History by its nature is revisionary.

Deliberate category errors are part of our make-up.
Mistaken identity is an evolutionary force.

The *odd kind of sympathy* between pendulums says like things pull at each other.
The root shows affection for its dark critters exhibiting themselves.
No animals in the museum.

What if the sense of being called home includes monstrous monstration?
I admit to trouble staring down everything that creates itself in me. They party in.
The dance is firing up the horizon.

When I go into the animal pushing up inside its kingdom subjects me.
Some permission fields are categorically strange.

I'm not brave—I'm trying to be funny.
Ai Weiwei

Language music, music language, no one knows whether or why not.
Except you say.
All charged words are orphans now.

Timing is a relation to not.
I say line and it says cliff.

The impossible truth about poetry is it just happens like it or not.
I am momentarily a page and you are my pen. You never get used to this.

Music does not teach here from there. Mind the gap.
The middle knowing itself is a vertical wedge in the present.
Writing is strategic space management where the surround is strange.

Are these raw wiggling showings not mine speaking of face value?
Malformation is unaccepted life.

History is the note last played, now forgetting itself but for a lingering feeling.
Timing is a relation to knots.
Birth defects as divine monstration is as good a thought as any out here in left field.

This is a poem in knowing that you are its reader and is conditioned accordingly.
I track you tracking in advance advancing our common ground.
Listening is radial like time presencing.

Self-strange entities, how can I object?
Music turns history's bad habit of repeating itself on its ear.
Communication is on the rebound.

Time to open inside the never before heard.
Love suffers its surfing poetics.

No things but in ideas (in *their* words not ours).

A line sounds to make up a neighborhood hoping to get along.
That one of these lingual tracks returns upon itself in one ear all tracks switch.
Collisions are inevitable in a reconfiguring world, its mind-degradable collusions.

Reading organizes swinging out to in.
Proliferating ears fall in arrears.
Everything doubles in troubling sound of mind and body.

Knowing you changes you. Me too.
And I don't mean who, what!
Hwaet!

Language doesn't know itself unless it says itself knowingly in you.
So many selves coil the wording.
Too few homophones foil the silent knowing.

Let us now not praise famous phonies. That's politics.
Our hero swordship sails the cutting ledge.
Our music is on loan from transtemporal natives committed to living on.

The unsayable invisible hides in the inaudible renamable.
History stumbles to stammer truer.
To engage this way is to enter the fray, olé!

An eagle cut low across our lawn today like the thought I thought impossible.

Today is trying to go on forever in releasing delight, last in deceasing forward.
Mourning disappearance takes too much present.

Feeling the great in the poem puts me to shame.
I reckon I enjoy a Southern origin.
Still no memory of expulsion from hortus conclusus—a vague breakout *may*be.

Music does not differentiate you from me, so poetry aspires to its condition.

To experiment is to try out the newly given.
Everything is learning wheels until the engine jumpstarts the driver.

Stir between ears to avoid sedimentation.
I hear you through fingers, you pulse.
Any moment now the poem reboots and the mind lights up.

Referents are coming in droves, time to sidestep.
I'm reading out of the corner of my eye this writing record of disjunctive sounds.
I'm finally able to follow what I don't yet know is there.

Did I see the eagle or merely sense the trace of its successful evasion?
Wake me up at the end of the line thus pointing out instruction in the dead book.
Poetry never entirely between covers is writing that lives again.

Only speaking to myself I don't know my communicant.
Music can't resist prompting eternity.

Sound stalks mind.
We are addicted to ourselves.
Concept procures, principle perdures.

Biography promotes voyeurism.

The music of the line is a set-up for anomia waking.
There is strange attractive force in a poem without readers.

Setting up mind *houses*.
There's an empty line waiting for me to move in on it.
Present hope is to cure the expectation of the good line for good.

Don't buy it.
Fiction heals.
Language so contained ferments.

I'm taking life in my hands to get a hold on this page a finger to point through with.
Body hears beyond the ears.
Music is sound fictioning.

A daemon doesn't know how to spell its name because writing is *our* business.
The work's as long as mind is long embedded.
Fiction cuts grooves that stay, same as any other real.

Imagine Creation with anything-for-a-good-joke at heart.
And just over here a new model travels bareback.
Infinitely singularly so.

The Master in the dream asked, Do you know what my favorite practice is?
I said No. Then he:
And then the men set foot on the land...

There's no today for all of our mañanas are wild right now.

The line dreams forth.
Every take a double take.
Feeling watched in sleep must be me trying to get back here, not knowing where.

Certain language lovers know Eros is hiding just under the verbal skin.
Mouth throws open the gates to tongue lashing letters.
Language forgets to be self-animating and then suddenly recalls.

Some words remember when they were young.
Reaching a point of realization that life at its truest is most truly indefensible.

Note the recurrent impulse to rescue the lost self inseparable from wild world.
Poetry returns us to the state of not being sure of what anything is.
The word is once again dipping down into itself buck naked.

My reverie revs.
The stream you can't step in twice twines the flow in what this knows.

Never defend or so pretend.
The poem is calling language back to own its obscure nostalgia for childtime.
The sound is keeping close to its issue.

Sounding *etymonym* names its verbum *wombing* that we home in on here.

Desire to relive one's life to get it right this time is as unavoidably recurrent as nuts.

Can I sound down to go inwardly around?
That's less a question than a wet finger in the air feeling where the wind slows.

I'm forever scouting out the land of the departed familiar souls.
Will dropping down through the word into root pools talk us into necroglossia?
Don't answer that, it's a cue.

Startle follows the true start.
What does it feel like saying what you don't dare say?
Here we are once again caught up in half-believing.

Sex staying mysterious reminds, the mystery is always.
Startled to be here.
Half-seeing, the voyeur zone, is the between of impossibles.

There are only alls in the realm of exposed.
You can't really *have* questions once you know you're inside the question.
The line dreams beyond the dreamer, persisting in its folly.

Here we are hoping for a helping hand to mouth.
Here we go round the mulberry bush.
Infinite singularity.

So pass me that other instrument.
I've got the itch to play badly.
Scratch the sound. Mind bleed.

I'm listening to the music of the unspoken.
Nevertheless I hear say your hearsay with each ear going its own way.

Everything is absolute as far as it goes.

So the new logic showing up on my so to speak doorstep is page specific.
A page is a poem waiting to happen, and your claim to being here is proof.
You get a line reshaping to include evanescence in the plural.

It alternates seeing and speaking and reading responds to a certain kind of touch.
The experience at hand is a function of reaching to the perceived end.
And the after flow *glow!*

Still it's getting harder and harder to believe I'm here where I seem to be.
The timeless time of the sentence is when grammar does not serve time.

I'm feeling the possible reading in the actual reading mind and its page turning.
It says what can't say this, yet it smells words like fingers.

I carry various amulets because I have trouble keeping my mind in the right gutter.
There's slippage on the imaginal slippery slope and its verbal equivalents.

The poetics of the rudder indicates this is where I don't want to go, and we're early.
It makes you move your fingers and you smell the coming aura and call it something.

Word DNA shows being knowing what it is that can't not be.
Speaking words teaching tongues sparks a species.
The place is only as good as its song.

If it happens it's non-negotiable.

Everything I've said to you heart to heart is stolen from the poem yet to come.

I can't see for seeing, she is saying inaudibly.

There's a poetics of the manifesto declaring what has always been still unseen.

Gender is consequential even among stones.

If the preverb claims to be female what motivates doubt between this and that?

A good question should work standing on your head.

Looking up quests.

Justice at last! Note the sound of her voice is not the irony you think.

She means refusing to play *to*.

Your training in emotion detection stands in the way of right genderation.

Happenstance alerts self programing to its singular edge, *you're on ledge*.

I'm studying the information coming from all around unbound.

Being long asks not how but where not, how not.

I'm still honing my willfulness to the discipline of reception.

And then the men set foot on the land…

Startle drives the dream back in.

Here it knows life never gets out of the middle of itself so why should our telling?

We need self aware moments to drive us over the edge.

All addiction is self addiction.

Love is all over. Hip to tip and over.

Here we are over the top—well, on top over itself.
Aiming to get beyond orientation based on directionality exclusive of between.
If only we could read end on back we'd feel at home in our homelessness.

I declare the right to rethink the world for all the good it will do me.
This is the real me speaking in the one language I still can't say I know.
Can't help hoping you can hear my heart beating as proof this page is alive.

News of my life has been greatly underreported, on purpose.
Lipstick on your color tells a tale on you is overreported as the nature of the beast.
This is the body of the beast by another color propensity, a heartfelt music.

And this effort protects against undercutting music's exact percipient fancy.
The inner curve of the dips in pulsation is what feeling follows to come into being +.
I never know what I just said until it tells me.

If you heard all the people quoting Shakespeare on Earth at any moment, a music.
Same way your whole life till now taken as the music of this moment, hardly audible.
The lyrics to this opera is the cry of your life broadsided by your philosophy.

Today I saw the trace of something that didn't happen and I pray never will.
I saw the body in the air following impact and the mind learning to fly overhead.
This seeing is reading the pulse as bedtime story.

It's the song of my life if it produces the effect still to register.
The deal at hand is with the Earth recovering from shock.

I can only say what I half believe is happening in the field.

I am fictional in my own account.
Identity is a status report.
Ah to be a good old-fashioned good-for-nothing.

Saying what you half believe proves dying is from the beginning.
I'd like to say get over it but I first have to get out from under the said and done.
A good line reports further on the half said.

When I think syntactic ambiguity I sense a sacred text is signaling mid-sentence.
Preverbs are readymades found in the shiftily lingual mind.
They talk about themselves to get us off their back.

That things can't help allegorizing is the basis of syntax or so the story goes.
Everything urges toward its lingual aura.
I objectify when you hear me, so we can move on together.

Caught in struggling neighbor mind I catch myself wiggling a way out.
I'm not asking you to think of this like the girl next door. I hear *furl neck store*.
Heroic projection withholds what excludes her. She lights up.

I'm not asking you to moor your houseboat here. Berth your gender afloat.
Respiration is beyond aggression, inspiration beyond repression.
Re: what you half believe, something inside wants the permission to say so.

The good new days are the good-for-unsayable.
There's an ecology of lines as of signs of minds beyond the good of *for*.
Terms are misnamed for they rarely end where they are.

I know the feel when the words belong on this page and no more.
One by one they carry the load just this far. Blood flow.

The words mean what they say whether I do or not.
The impulse to make begins as attachment so I wonder *make from release of same?*
Never assume you know what you mean let alone them.

Terms accommodate their occasion and ambi-valence is high-speed oscillation.
Thinking walks in the park and swims in the sea at once indifferently.
I'm asking that you hear me out and then back in.

If the body is as readable as visible it's as visible readable as audible.
If to hear it is to fear it we should listen up. Back up.
Feedback listens back to the present as if back to the future.

This is an experiment in knowing how the present knows that it is.
Philosophy begins when you forget who thought it even if you think it was you.
This runs counter to received wisdom and by this I mean this.

Our companions are far between the few and so lonesome feelings are birthright.
I'm intently aiming at something that won't be the same when I get there, or here.
The poem is the present we're still never been to.

Thought is neither tasteless nor odorless and words are their own weight.
And it's not afraid to talk about itself as if it existed.
The body that is.

---

[2] Baruch Spinoza

Whoever wrote this book did me a big favor letting me claim it.
Desire shakes everything back down to itself.

Presuming meaning extends the sense of the real willy-nilly.
Reading on the take from the past misses the oncoming mind.
I've been listening in circles.

Time won't think away.
Identity is a progress report.
Who are we but they who do not sweep their ecstatic free zones under the rug.

In the healing tent consciousness goes in and out of writing.
Real discipline is founded on affection and attraction.
Hearing is coming to before impact.

Self-thinking thoughts do not go gently into preferred thought slots.
It could all no doubt be said more simply but then it wouldn't be itself.
Hearing how you feel like doing does it.

Hey good lookin' striates across the eardrums.
Yet affection for realized likeness parties with attraction to the possible true.
Now raw what's cooking.

A new sound gets a chokehold and no way's legal.
The musical miracle's sub-quotable.
All day I've been looking everywhere for my endangered disparity (cf. *agent arity*).

It all runs along on the long smooth runway to nowhere.

It starts in the feet to misspell ground *irruptameter*, the literal beat *up*.
Present text is a world finding itself complete saying itself for once and now.
This registers the register on the far side in the outer fold within hearing.

The fact of my disagreement with myself is invariant.
Incarnation is the space force of words leaping out of their knowns.
A thing lives commanded to know its meat.

The fate of the text is none of its business.

Identity stepping back from itself regresses outward openly.
Other names call from lost opportunity in ongoing pre-existence.
Sorry if this sounds irreal, that's its calling card.

It won't talk to me if I sweep its wyrdness under the rug.
The only reader is the one who wants it to be herself.
There's drift in the inner conversation and a pull to her propriosonic phonic current.

Gender overspecifies even while forking.
Phoning home with all her unheard voices.
First responder poem rushes to what most urgently might have been, still calling.

The integrity is in the sticktoitiveness in sliding vowels hauling heavy fractalics.
I think she means syntactic fracking so to speak earthly and desperate.
This calling itself registerial inlays her antic messaging head cracking philogics.

It can't help saying what's never been said strictly under its own pressure.
Let's step over here in the corner and let it all go by.

The passing mind doesn't know what to do laying back and riding the tide.
It sounds its own entwine.
Twirl syntactics automatically tongue test some syllables, it relieves to know.

Loosening the grip the words are going into a slide.

A scrying dowsing handholds the gaps between.
A shape conflates its unseen trails, old friends now feral.

Beware of incantonics.

The poem is the tongue in its own cartoon.
It's reading the cards it lets go calling.
It spits its music and slates back the dying fall to ground itself.

That brain again and cranial slush knows life again in strain.
Allegorical refrain means holding back on story until it shows its lacks.
A poem makes no promise to mean what you mean by mean. Raw means.

Eros borders.
The textured surface figures siding over.
The hoards we let enter are just returning home from the wars I mean shores.

A god invents poetry to get off his rocker.
Temporary benefits are rocket effects.
Any minute now I'll know why I said this even while listening before.

Take it all away in time to make space for meaning unforewarned.

My bad handwriting is final proof of my bad education expressed badly here & now.
Poetics is stand-up gratitude in disguise.

As you know from word one it's deadly serious to the bone.
Taking life as a trial balloon you may lean toward poetry as scripture.
Even writing in disappearing ink there are traces detectable by good forensics.

I remind myself it is not essential to recognize my own voice.
Solitary kledomancy proves strays are everywhere and meaning inevitable.
We are looking through a glass darkly with empiricist passion.

The drive to tell all haunts.
I turn my back to the edge waiting for the page to turn.
Text is tale texture with telling tincture—divination by t's.

I'm (not) just making this up.
Title: *My Daimon Does Dirty Dancing Behind My Back*
The ecstatic M.O. is a dead giveaway taken literally.

The mind you find in the anomalous text has eluded you till present and never was.
The poem writes in the present future.
I mean every word that doesn't mean itself first.

Freedom from anxiety acts verbal before neural.
I'm catching my act by the motto *leap before you look.*
Rejoice from tall buildings while there are words to spare.

Our good sentence gets us nowhere fast and well before the end in sight.

I'm signaling you from afar because we're beings who signal.

How to see in a word who signs?

The poem is attempting to find out what life wants from this page.

The higher presence for want of word.

The figure afar afire aware flares.

Where the tongue trips is the hold.

Verbal vertigo comes of flutter in high tones.

Music does not teach here to there. Mind its back.

Education only happens in gaps.

The waver in the moan is the psyche's loan tone.

Obsessing self-timing measures in laps.

You know when word is wanting by the sing in your ears.

Presence has amplitude whose high hits happiness ambi-/equi-valently.

How you handle ending tells all in aftermath.

The trail follows the grain down as mown.

I'm minding all this as afterflow with glow.

Muscle tones in tuning up as lineaments inspire.

Citation is behind itself as lost in hope to quote a future.

Rime is about the selfsame no escape of rounding.

Float the loan that hears you home.

Venus rises in halves of the angles you know her from.

Decision splits you off trail.

My resistance to seeing the whole moment is proof I was born dual and it's not over.

The first moment of the rest of your life is a wavering thought ... less true ... not.
So we have to return here to read our way back to where we start.
It keeps happening over and over and it's not even itself.

The great visionary texts that undermine religion are reintextated in the undertow.
I worship at the shrine of deformational images.
They look at me with the *e y e* with which I look at them.

The song is holding in on small groups of phonemes.
The mode of concatenation is a secret held in the open.
So watch the word god attract its majuscule and dance high germanic syntactics.

What draws us to think the unthinkable? Ledge logic.
My images and I co-blink.
Leap before you slip.

Poem awaits its unborn reader to cut through to unreveled unrevealing.
Rime is sound bounding around its own bounce hitting its wall.
Poetic crime is deformation. Laurels available. Music.

Once it starts it's impossible to run out.
If I rime I'm going dumb like the idiot I'm learning to be.
Time chimes in the place of the word.

We're just falling around, no resistance, and thick air.
Metalistening allows you to disengage without leaving the scene of the crime poem.

You have to want to get from here to there going nowhere fast enough to resist slide.
I might say the poem is pushy because it won't brake for my small animal thinkings.
To get the feel you have to imagine you're inside a runaway train moving too slowly.
Pull the emergency brake and the music gets louder.

The peripeteia is the jolt to the end of the current car.
I learn falling around with uncharacteristic joy.
It will be time to chime as *poem* no more when I achieve full-bodied forgetfulness.

We're working out a many cars theory re: our habit of working out of many cars.
These very cars we're living in whose sounds mask neuronic discharge.
(Give me a moment while we connect with an alternate stream.)

Possible rhythmos with forked footing.
It lies until you stop deciding.
What's true is your shoe.

Forth is backwards and even roundabout co-depending.
Polyhedron plane faces a step beyond two-faced.
Self-proving is lifelong.

A journey's as long as mind is long embedded.
Occurring discourse is recourse uncovering the glossological event in progress.
Now for a break to vent our stored longing for the garden of earthly delights.

Reading presumes sentience.
The langue in tongue makes the slaver waver.
Green fuses in the fresh eye seeing through.

It feels I'm surfing the pulsations entraining.
The mind asks permission to go whole hog.
We're experiencing weather in the timing saying.

Passionate contortion is a trick of tongue.
Music is usage.
Force of a vision rouses continuance.

You wouldn't be hearing I wouldn't be saying if lingual logic didn't let up in time.
Seeing clear through is seeing at all in these halls.
Synecdoche in everything is saying anything.

The surface hardens with frequency of pass through.
The shine can be blinding.
The practice in view is self-deepening minding.

Needing to interpret what's at hand frames a human need to manipulate.
Good poetry is for people used to trying to please.
The word god is leaning toward anarchy.

Rising to the line level loses all handles.
Harder to remain where you are the more it is here.
Tough things never tire of coming to the surface.

I appeal for the return of attitudes lost between groupings.
Homage to ghostlier remark demarcations.
Passé instantly.
This can be said once only in the time of its saying.

Original sin is first self-awareness gone south.
Half ate the fruit, half went off.
I'm judging, no escaping the fact, and granting amnesty as fast as I can run.

A line is a focus you make or not yet moving on is living on.
All secrets are ambivalently embedded before bedtime.
Attitudes are passé instantly.

Flashing red lights remind my prayer to interrupt me.
The testimonies are life edging over.
The snake under my mind impurifies to lure, *holy holy*.

Now I'm caretaking the half-eaten fruit.
Perhaps I am a formalist as if paraformalist were real.
If it proves free being it has poetics.

We're here driving the change in names. Mary Holy Mary contrary.
I was hurt it was thought the attitudes mine in all this vanishing.
Concept is immaculate conception in art mind.

Only asking you enter the zone of this thought.
Listen up the poem responds to the question of the possibility of poetry at all.
It leaves us behind at the drop of a that.

A rime in time is the idiot level sounding itself out.
Hear or fear fall.
No not making up stories to fit the crime.

Good days are good lines in the sand and the wind is blowing.

Stepping on the center is walking on your belly through life.
Experience is an absolute until interpreted.

How many of me are there is syntactic.

There are no better or worse numbers but the configure powers.
Words choose verbing as humans gender.
First person is Adamic and the singular verbs.

It gets lonely in here with none of our favorite people.
Make up your numbers as you go, now go by.
A thing has its principle in stride.

Reading is off the hook.
Life like the poem knows what it's doing even if I don't and I don't.
Like the line like an endless conversation this is in the beginning.

The date is number making it up as it goes, absolutely.
Sooner or later you understand something and then the trouble begins.
Talking rimes with stomach gurgling.

Syntactic cliffhanging after a while feels like flying.
All the same the poem cannot know itself but it is known.
A letter is a sound uttered only.

Throwing my arms around doesn't prove surround but I feel it.

Language is a terrain and the tongue is haptic.

It is prefigured to refigure the following and following.
The poem knows what is being said irreally to the poet.
If you allow yourself to figure the listening it speaks to you with your own mind.

I write for the extremes of attention in a possible reader on whom depends a future.
Sincerity includes leaving the holes where they are.
Declaring isn't claiming.

I'm excited it hits me it's never been said to excite me.
Standing in the way of language you get impact at the edges mid body.
Likewise music is manual even when hands free.

Refining mind gets physical.
Feeling fingers get cuts midsentence.
Keeping my hands to myself is solipsistic verbal behavior.

When I say she I mean god sometimes and sometimes goddess and then there's her.
The problem of identity is the same on mountain peaks and unnamed planets.
Saying so seeds the night while solving nothing.

The poem waltzes to its end as a dance to the death.
Comic grotesque leveling danse macabre duende leaves no man standing.

I declare I'm claiming even less than this.
A text is sacred only on the days it's on.
It puts you on, it turns you on, it knows you on, off, at once.

eternal discomfort of the heavenly bent

for Kimberly Lyons & Vyt Bakaitis

Out here in the space whose name is on the verge of showing a pulse:

I'm in a state of panic and I'm taking to the page.
My words are numbered like my days but with less accumulation than bounce.
Yet my days are flooding behind and the words flowing ahead. This is the spread.

The dance of death and the dance of birth are getting it on.
Gypsy flamenco dancer spits on watchers slinging her dying song.
In the economy of always last words I'm betting the house on the breath.

The only emotion sustained comes with conviction unconvincing a notch up.
We've passed the point where seduction contains.
Time to scale the page rappelling from line to line.

The poem returns to teach the mind self-conversing language with a hitch.
Polylinguality is mixing in the roots.
It ties your tongue to a toothy twist resuscitating mouth to mouth.

Not getting sucked into canon construction's more anti-church than anti-war driven.
Or maybe not.
The avant-garde is block by block. And alphabet showing.

Every island is a man and gendered oceanic.
Intelligence encloses.
I'm inside mind where thoughts draw down.

Thinking weathers.
Not sure how we got here but everything is getting pulled into place.

Duck! The lines are coming from all angles.
Reading is covert action for an unknown collection agency.
Paying dues as saying does.

Language is repelling communication in favor of self-unmarked communiqué.

Love this movie life, hate the movie, can't wait for the end, over too soon.
I'm tracking history a line at a time by the nano pulse.
Timeline follows radial trying to keep up with film fate radical.

Number's where calculation and angelic incursion stare each other to a standstill.
Stand with the greats to keep your ego in place.

"Art neurosis is the consequence of teaching according to people's opinions."
Clearing the issue up is also out and away. Expect confusion. Words switch frames.

Brain is a dwarf synecdoche for mind.
Pray next life to be a brainy bitch of indeterminate color, codename: Dakini.
This is a disguise for willfully fluctuant gender in the Klein bottled wild. Scent wins.

Jump around with me and fling your spitting image straight up.
Akashic notetaking scratches a future like cavewall racehorse in the third.
Trust only what's out of school.

The attack is over my head. The content is none of my business.
Poem now's a site awarding points for a good fumble. Defining good.
The aim is loosing true anarchy upon the world so we can think natural.

I've got this object-like entity on my tongue turning itself into a wordflow.
Its racket synesthesizes colorfully and with just enough surface friction to turn on.
Like turning on a dime, turning to proto-sublime, wringing rime from comfort tone.

Tongue learns to love the things it does worst.

Therefore no therefore.
If I call you here as real I take you apart to a part.

Self is only a theory.
Eternal return is the intensive vision of infinite variation.
Either way you don't see it happening.

Language is a placeholder with holes and the trick is holding the place hole open.
Everything pulses in the grand audition.
We're talking skin here.

I am concretely sure.
Skip telling me who I am and I you.
Name transports identity, think *paramesia* or the moth that sounds psychotic.

Bio-logos is rough going and at a given point has a sound as poignant as scent.
It's equal to an opening in the rain forest, a field of fungi, a zone clear to gather in.
It's preverbial if autotrophic, makes its own food, nurture words up from undertime.

Mind twist word torque letteristic turn into *paramecia* or words oblong alongside.
The translation is the ride inside more surface than psychosis.
We're coming up for air bearing in breath the thingly wish to show up.

The plot is how you track the gaps.
Mind recalls letting the bottom fall out between words. Calling up bottoming out.

Draw down her untimed mind complex into syntax complex at your own risk.
Bach is rethinking my ear at a distance, spaceless.
Space knows it is just pretending.

To say she has magic is practicing what you preach.
Any edge is singular.
I've got a toe up on the ledge supposing legibility and so I hold up this zeroing sign.

Understanding is overrated.
Any rating is over the top edge.
I keep trying to say there's never enough nothing. Substantially little at that.

Pretend you're hearing this in a bar like an abstract expressionist downtown.
Signifying nothing sound and fury and all the rest of culture is turning biological.
Fungal from the jungle bio logos trying to tell all by what lives at the dying edge.

Listening up writing down gives just enough topos logos to keep us on our feet.
Words hug the syntax that makes them feel real.
Switch grammar midline to prove you're not a tree.

Correction: There is no proof for real things.
You just see what talks.
It takes hands on to take place among the faithful.

Believe only what you see when you're not sure your eyes are open.

I toe the line that tows the words up a hill of beans for a meaning to come.
What's happening is absolute until interpreted.

What matters but to put it on the line.
Innuendo intended with coming suspended.

Poetry makes no promise to keep you feeling good. Bad neither.
I draw the line to make self-reworking syntax free to hold the chaos.
It talks about itself the way you talk about yourself so you know you're still there.

Meanwhile it's looking for its other name.
Still, names make no promise to be who is said.
Longing attracts all new escape routes.

Homesickness is a withdrawal symptom in a life of addiction to life.
Escapism hacks the operating system to mess with mother code.
What you call esoteric I call hide and seek.

Discomfort or rather non-comfort pervades the holy land imagined.
It wants me reading from the gaps.
Gonna sit right down and write myself a letter./And make believe it comes from you.

I decline reclining on the hit bottom.
Time to kick the habit on the edge of the rabbit hole.
I'm learning to get the feel of the updraft locating the way to say.

Its only promise is keeping going.
Any moment practices showdown.

You say accidental rhythm and I say footfalls regaining balance.
Ring the bell to make it tell itself.
We live on cue given the other who.

Fun is absolute until called out.
Saying no closes hearing.
This float takes hold on the go.

No show no flow.
Nothing to lose but your refrains.
Riming with trains always says there is more.

She takes being knowing self comes looked at.
Modeling soul first.
History futures in the show she shows up. The who.

Now let's get down to basics on all fours.
Real structure is matrix attracting acts as fingers knowing how to find herself.
I write ex——tensions and feel the tension contends me out.
I remember incorrectly, I correct, now two truths live forever in mind.

My past is always still happening.
Steps and missteps and resteps, trip *up*.
Home stretches in the home stretch.

Retaining trace is the way the race knows itself.
I live the historical phantasy I last beyond this.
Hysterical life fan I repent at long last to seriously study her fun love.

Looking outback at the walnut tree I am seeing back into my cells.
Modifiers covering the life addiction, it's dangling all over.
The critical point of knowing anything truly organizes differently.

Middle flush sounds syntactic.
A poet hangs from his lack until read. Saved in the nick!

Let's go sliding along the newest grooves until they cut clear through.
Aim disallows hitting the target.

The hand that reaches before me reaches for me.
Fooling love is the Fool doing living.
At root poetic means crazy talk with practice.

Bring in the dog and take out the cat. (refrain)
Culture keeps its self identity living inside language at any given person's expense.

Compassion has no thought, no moral.
As the waiting gap is widening we live longer inside.

Mind dangles faster than the grip on language.
Feel everything at once.

My lips are trying to form something heard yet never recalled yet still calling.
Poetry is the feedback no one remembers requesting.

Feel anything never once. You dare care. Things becoming go backwards.
As I sense time breaking down a new plane covers the top layer of my world.

Rethink time.
A storm's brewing already pushing up under my writing hand reaching for its kvass.
The fate of your name is the poem of your life. Ferment.

I am seeing eating.
At long last a self importance fast.

Prehended upended—the truth is life awkwardly situated and all over at once.
The poem is the language doing its living forever wherever.

Stand where you are, I hear said from down under, and a new reflex self births.
You got two hands to read your two grains of wood.

Not knowing where we're going we're free to hear in the round.
You say space I say time let's get the whole thing on.

I'm so far from master of my work the practice is looking elsewhere.

Just today the writing wriggled toes and left the expectation of rising beyond.
Dionysus has to get a start somewhere bodily and some one.

Poetry as reality's ruse is one of many ones.
It says a poetics is calling for the willing suspension of reading relief.

Flipping syntax retreads the cumulative trauma you never see coming.
The stormy brew bursting surface under the reading's still learning to talk.

The throat is an earth hole long like a well and tall like a tale.

And it means what it says to you.

The pronoun is up to you is how she survives being it.
Levels switch most when you're not looking.

There is no same but we know it.
The line is a site of unanticipated rumble.

One day you're reading and the tables turn on you.
Under the book, under the plate, under calculation.
Language moves toward an absorption state where one word flies many flags.

We can't stop surjecting.
Speaking of species a principled concept is a mental convenience with a bite.
I can barely manage my thinking in *ands*.

It's all in what we catch on to passing through.
I hear true when it hits from an unseen angle.
The free center sucks you into yourself.

Where does it all come from asks equal to *where does it all go*.
Glasses, tunnels minding enhances to see out as it is.
Any embedding saying is with treads.

You choose fusing.
Taste defrauds us daily.
The poem hungers like a hawk stooping.
Quick turn down.

Why can't I learn what I think I know?
All you can do is ask.

Time to add thinking in hawk.
The lifelike line in progress pools in the mind middle.
Mood swirls and muddle whirls. This is its story.

Loving embrace and eyes opening on a cactus. What kind?
Armful mindful.
Species is unstable like the notion it is.

Middle has voice only we forget in ordinary trance.
Relating weaves.
Believing is just one of the things to do.

Talk funny long enough you expect scripture.

It's only a poem when you say so. And then only now.
My contract says you only get to be what is projected for the time of its telling.
She tells me how to read it on the edge of not reading.

I'm just helping it know herself.
Not writing I don't know how to read.
My addiction is flagging her down with all my hands, as inherited.

Undercalculation leaves things be.
Writing gets me my guide for the day to come.
Sooner or later the author reveals how she means as in hawk.

Let's say *serving the page that serves her* as something meant.

We're building the bent as we go.
The ladder we climb is both ways at once.

We're crossing the plane of politic identizing in that speaking happens between.
Electric buzz or the part you feel fluxes.

Justification won't do.

To believe in God or not puts belief ahead of the pack, but it's still a pack.
Mental options run in packs.

I can't escape the feeling I have better things to do.

And and and and is never a brand.
At best it grabs me on the go and you go too.

No end to restruction.
Watching out for wobble to not be part of what you topple.

The world is the gap between two sounds.

I sense how long I've been conscious reaching back.
Syllable by syllable the world runs in.

Magical practice acts on the belief that something is there for you.
Saying it is its matrix.

Tonight I speak to you in Sherlock's voice running out on a religion of rationality.
The woods tastes in my fungus tea.
Every now feels like itself.

One space relates to another space by mirroring through the fence.
A magic carpet is a gravity-defying weave.
The thing written knows itself through you on either side of the fence.

Jacob's ladder is a surject with torque.
Buddha was no Buddhist.
Even counting gets you nowhere.

The tangle of refs is a vine around your ankles.
Your poem has a mind of her own.
She uses my brain to torque the wrangle.

Everyone is a believer even if only in not believing.
There is play in the fears.
Everything deserves its day in sport.

To know who's pulling the strings you have to take attendance by the nano sec.
Playless work makes Jacob a fall guy.
Modifiers dangle like her old lace, and the name walks free.

Everything ever said templates its moment of fame and shames to renew.
I believe what I say and the end of the line is the end of belief.
So I believe.

The element of surprise is the weight of the first word.
The map flaps under the breath.

Poetic extremes map human extremities.
Script scripture literature letter litter. Set of no order.

The sea rises with the force of breath.
Saying things like this we reach toward the other side.
Only a statement you could never believe in stands a chance of speaking over.

A parabolic line of thinking has personal trajection.
It's a throw.
It lands. It retains its trace as a way of holding the sky.

A life past or a passed life has a fragrance as afterflow.
A people is a forest and a family is a garden. Growing sets.
One word many sets a sentence verb optional. Verbal pervasion.

The present set is a certain saturation and quick evaporation.
Resetting changes state to the quick.
Anything said maps a bardo.

Grammar tracks the edges to go over.
Talking over the edge maps up to the next edge and over.
There is no end to over.

It's never over.

I'm all surface here.
Straight talk has trouble on the curves.

Writing is a hearing aid for meaning at a distance.
The dimension as magic carpet pulls itself out from under.
It's never fully for you without a climb.

The bardo of writing is a set all the way over.
The story is I lied in saying story.
It starts out true and by the time it gets to the lips it's lying for you.

I'm discovering learned ignorance.
It balances the vexation by thought of verbal immortality.
The celebrated accumulation of merit is a short dig down in living dirt bliss.

I strip down to the next level of morality play.
Just drama mama.
Bracket this space while an opinion passes through. Breathe. Now fire.

When a dakini shows up in paint my eyes learn figuring through the body.
Duende with roses and violets.
Gross listening risks going sacred naked.

We weave in waves.
I mean its telling me goes under before over.
Last best masks blow over rising up falling.

Not finding what is looked for looking.

Fold goes both ways.
Like when I get complicated explicating I imply pleating.
Thought gets hot under the collar.

Urge turns theurgic at the drop of a that.
The religio merges with the ligature.
If you knew it was the oracle you wouldn't mind the implications.

The darkening turns lighten the display.
Story is always a cover.
Light the pipe, Sherlock.

Letteristically flying is a lie lining covering going over.
And I promise you a rose garden in every line.
Just take me by the and.

She's showing me sheer variety of variability.
The Orphic radio is blaring in the i's.
Gender render is whatever she says he says it says.

We're now passing by an alternative and.
When I said fold the lie was cast and everything that follows is waves, no holding.
Who's behind this turn of events depends on the float view.

Fire in the hold.
Jet-propulsive words are nobody's fault.
Choose again if you have half a chance.
[*Authorization stopped before the present which is said to go without.*]

Language is always trying to tell us we don't know how it means.
For a person who has language language is synonymous with life.
The two words can't leave each other alone.

For an indeterminate span I rethink my life as a bridge from nowhere to nowhere.

"I don't know what you're selling but you're selling something." [D. Antin]
I realize I'm selling finding out what there is to sell.
So far I'm coming up empty-handed. I stay broke for the span.

If you know my meaning you've found me out.
You read me, I study you.
I'm here to take something away without saying what.

It can go either way means tragic and comic options stay open till the end.

If similar moments show up as one moment time stops dead.
If all moments are singularities, infinity's in no time.

This way of thinking is a function of altitude in overlooking.
We come into the world linked while forgetting.
Recall what you see when you're not sure your eyes are open.

Remember forgetting.

Please pass the talking pen.
Everyday I pass some time shaking my head at how much time has passed.
I live in the past except for now.

Before now there is no before now.
This is how I know I was born to laugh and cry.

Shaking loose of accumulating life rimes is a rite of passage.
The head out the window takes in air at its own risk.
This is the life.

The poem imitates life in knowing you want to revise it and it's resisting.
Infinite unassisted variation is its best hope.
You are seeing from an angle never guessed.

Even thinking about it confuses direction and necessity.
Time to skip over the non-understanding and feel the breeze of reason free.

Still making my way with learned ignorance.
You can never say when turning into your opposite begins.

Reading keeps in the foreground to ignore the ground doing the talking.
Sooner or later you tell all.
It makes sure.

Life never stops talking about being its own end.
I'm complicitous by default but the brain is shaking in its roots even as we speak.
A great turn has the force of a page ending and now for the wondering.

> *One eye sees, the other feels.*
> Paul Klee

My body the impatient child has been making faces out the rear window again.
The puppet absorbs the hand.

I was unable to sleep because my children still unborn are crying around here.
Feeling at home at last in the nest with the feast that is nowhere.

You are what you eat what you love what you are.
Being ends in itself which is here.

What gets called true experience is knowing itself on the backside of awareness.
Not resolution of issues but stepping into the next possible view.

Taking a shine to the sun is a moon thing.
We're just filling in spaces with what's missing.

The hand speaks in its puppet.
Great to see patterns knowing the source is elsewhere and now.

Modes are roads.
We're on the receiving end.
If you get with it you trip.

The fall from space is time invariance.
Try one on, tie one on, lie your way out of here.
Time on on—miswriting is the carpet aloft.

Even the rapidly passing is a constraint allowing a world.
Atwirl the voice amiddle.

I admit I'm hearing things.
Everything has edges still edging.

I keep poems happening so I have something to study.
The feeling is of being studied.

Obey the principle while representing nothing, that is the friction.
Life ends here where the affliction fractals on and on.

You can't see it which is why goddess made sensing.
Celebrating the birth with cactus in hand.

Images of the truth, sayings ontononymous, mouthfuls bigger than the head round.
You couldn't see it coming which is why it comes.

They who incarnate for a good laugh meet the wisdom in their way.
Their time is in recovery where there's no hope of recovery.

This is where you undergo the undergone.
To say it so is the further warp.

The lines lie in waiting in the motivated weave.
The discipline by intensity's still dealing with weak knees.

The performance performative of its own moment is nuance before image.
Replete relation is thread baring all.

If it's a tale it's tall and you *fall* for it.

The trip is trapping the will to hold in, gently, light touch, and waking relational.
To get on the inside with a winding center yet keep contact with the ground below.
It's all terrain and the rhythm frictive for the willing tongue so to say in place.

We dip in to get the words wet yet waiting for the inside to show.
You have to imagine an enchanted forest lighting up the syllables that dream you.
A universe goes feral on cue.

Not making sense is a placeholder.
Restraining before the swirly gate is a sexy between.
Any time through is self true if you come to(o).

We're talking the thing done together.
I'm here as long as the thing comes through.
A thing has a ring like a phone voice.

Person is a tone among tones.
A thing is known on a slant.
You feel the mind brushing up against you.

The aquarium whale looks on, sees into you, feeling thinking, like us.
Judge him by the level of self rebuilding the seen through.
Scant rant goes silent in the sense of trap.

Disconnection is a species of connection.

Seeing acting living at a distance characterizes life beyond mirrors.
Everywhere if anywhere.

probing or burrowings in all directions
Artaud

The face here is what can't face what it can't see.

I'm wearing a mask to emphasize it's not me you're seeing on extended ear.
The language is so new I get to speak it without cues.
Disconnection hunts down the suppressed allowable connection.

Once said it's obvious. Hints add up. Meaning piles. And when the wind blows…
The hand juts behind the back to catch in real time.
You can almost feel her lips finding their way into your spine to have a word.

We only travel back roads.
What you think back here distributes in the field before reaching you.
The teaching is the tracking from the soles out … no end.

I dream the Allapattah preacher hitting hard brimstoned syllables barring sense.
I'm surrounded sounded. This is what it means to be very very young.
From the beginning is the sound down under me—in the key of me!

The path is hearing itself through you *who—who can't say who.*
It confuses you with the you who sounds.
A person tones and we tune.

Not getting religion you get poetics so you say gnoetics to get more who than you.
From conceptual immaculate conception to principled penetration, still no who.
Just now learning to talk to myself in my absence. Late floomer.

Our days are numbered but not in order.
The feedback to come is in denial about reversal.

There's a kind of script they hand you that makes you a scribe.
No doubt the evidence extends to the tombs. The inscribed dark.

There are secret ands to the backroads in even ordinary linguality.
A certain art consists in letting the turns take themselves.
You know it happens when you're standing different.

Words show up knowing themselves—they have that look in their eyes.
Not a consistency but a lucency.
This means recognition not by familiarity but rightnowness all the way.

Reading is a subset of eyes mattering to mind without the distinction open/closed.
You can go to a meeting in the electric dark.
The hands are touching an own world address unknown.

It's only here not knowing how to say so.
Syntax proceeds by pushing back.
And pushing self away loses heat.

Someone else is in this room.
You can almost smell the words unsaid.
It reads to you even though it goes right past you.

Slow down something is crossing the road.
The point is not to hit the fleeing object.
There's an incontestable spread on the underside of space.

To notice this space is to find another there right there between.

Whereas overload is from the beginning a signal to ease in.
You know it's really happening when the frisson stirs the body physics.
You can't say what has gotten into you.
You say so unreasoningly bold.

No one will be watching us in the present unlit road.
Undertime traveling is only late before the time is known.
Starting time never comes and never isn't.

You have to use that tone of voice when no one's listening.
If you hear it you know it's for you without being meant for you.
A primordial disappointment has to go sit in the corner.

You begin to feel you've been left alone on purpose.
The rendezvous is prearranged unspecified.
All names have had their license temporarily suspended.

The words mean what they say until further notice.
We're trying to get in on their conversation as we speak.
No one tells us anything at any point until we know they're telling all.

Conspiracy has the wrong register like conniving for an alternative heartlessness.
There's a middle say in the inevitable muddle.
Riddled minds link alike.

I can get spooked when it touches me another way.
Confession can get distracting so I'm moving on to the unending page.
The burden of reading is saying when.

Who can refuse the offer of a warm body at the end of the phrase?

You are young again whenever the world makes no sense but sensing in all senses.
Poetic logic has the option of no logic at all.
When you hear language you keep trying to find the person in there.

Keep looking for ways to explain not being St. Francis in the wild.
Floom! is the sound of your engine trying to incarnate.
This has nothing to do with puzzling.

I've stopped waiting for the first shoe to drop. May the second precede.
I never get used to the writing knowing what it's talking about when I don't.
Lean on thee or some other presumed support literarily. Not.

I'm still here because it started making sense when I squint.
Free of the me in the mirror.
None the poorer for the furor.

Truth is a matter of mood where mind matters.
Then we come to substance and reality incubation.
Not much call to love the world back and yet you feel it coming between fingers.

Thrice worn. Feeling down. Taking it all off and putting it all on.
We go bare to touch our world in the right parts risking all.
Maybe haven't given up arguing to give up arguing.

Goodbye to all that … audience response.
A good curtain never finishes dropping.

Even being here in the room I'm getting ahead of myself.
Life is the trap looking like a trap door.

Poem is the stage of language moving mind from one room to another.
Preparation is for bigger rooms ahead.
The door reads *that said* to discourage the finisher from opening.

No room in the rooms for lounging. Tight flit.
The space is the stage of language laughing to keep letters apart.
You are who you beat.

Hence the unloved unloving uncalling world called *mine*.
You can think your way into a hole but not necessarily out.
The talk is happening to keep us studied.

At each instant the mind decides meaning or no.
Is anyone there, is anyone home?
Neighborhood goes dark. And there was dark.

The poem makes no promise to draw conclusions nor to withdraw in time.
Pushing on without pushing form.
The birth death zeugma is the befuddlement of *is*, verb transtransitive.

A line is to be used or losed.
The only reading is misleading.
Folding body at the end of rime is the suprasegmental long foretold.

It takes forever to get through where voice fleshes out in feeling tones.

There are musics too unusual to use until now is back.

You start out meaning one thing and find out meaning is another.
It got into your body not looking, still dangling, precisely.

Meaning is absolute or not at all.
The same as the handhold to or falling.
I had my fingers on the keys and then they turned around.

I'm already late for the performance that hasn't begun without me.
I'm thinking Bach stripped percussioning to the record no one recalls but me.
If certain sounds didn't exist without proof I wouldn't be me. They may say I'm not.

Life has likeness even without liking.
Free center still sucks you into yourself no escape.
Even the keys will talk to you.

She dances difference inside any one turning out many.
Gender decides a value without telling you.
Any given moment has just so much body.

Not every day is a day without eagles.
One absolute after another with its ups and downs.
So many trying out being per syllable fattens senseless and percussive.

You're picking up on going on never promised. Music!
Mind is seeking protection in some unfamiliar places.

There are muscle sinews too unmusical to lose now back on track.

A poem is absolute incursion even coming at all.
You find the meaning of having your name.
Words possess.

There are strings instrumental as nerves.
Looking one way it's coming another.
Listening in brings change to the hearing thing.

The level is the long wait.
Nothing pretends prehending.
These are words startling themselves for no reason yet gathering.

The voice is stringing as words fingering.
You can't have thought itself before.
I learn as I slow in the faster feet.

I'm warned not to take aim except lying.
Prone is a state of truth.
It doesn't know its own tone until it folds.

Not writing, won't stay alive.
The mode in denial seeks both oblivion and ecstasy.
Pain is one of the edges.

She smiles surgical.
Sink into the body at wave surge where the tip cuts you out.

In the dream she showed me her vocal sinews.
She said don't look so hard you'll see your ideology staring back.
I'm just now registering the lure to think about what can't be thought about.

Sticking to a meaning the words accused the reader of lexical adultery.
I'm learning how it feels sitting on this spot.
Mode shifts into medium to let the wild flight mood find its stray sinews.

Muscle relying on feedback from bone takes this spare time to tone you.
Were staring at your navel being blocked by the navel orange you're clutching[?]
Grammatical mood is getting moody.

A poem is time spared.
A thought has a tune.
Corruption in life or tone or digital file ruins function.

Music delays the inevitable indefinitely in the moment.
Am I even functioning when the line unfolds?
In the dream she postponed joy until she could come down to its level.

Form suddenly is the slippage in repeated numbers.
Proof it's alive is its resistance to premature recognition.
Poem were its function of crossing dimensions.

I'm proving I'm here this once. Poof.
Speaking without your tone isn't speaking.
And there was tune.

In the dream I had to write the enlightening inscription on line in time in matter.
The ground is hungry to pulse receiving from me as foreground in hover mode.
It's not part of doing to know what you're doing.

The reading puppet beats me to the lip.
Knowing in doing is not what.
Her eye names burning through this very spot.

The alternative self is studying me in writing here.

The problem with reflection is staying too long it jumps the gun.
Would that every word be its meaning or instant feed feeding back further.
The beast is in the mirror.

Beauty recoils from the syllable laid waste by not declaring the bond.
It's impossible to know what you mean meaning what you know.
There's an echo in here but whose voice?

Things done extremely for themselves are the things done multiversal.
I feel overlay of head her voices hold the space around in.
I'm told it's personal when the threshold has excessive moisture.

Three questions beginning who do we write for?
Continuing mid mind who does one write for?
And finally reaching me who do I write for?

Straddling the argument is a leg over option.
Whom's.

We're on the verge of desisting from ordinary presence.
Hold my hat, there's wind to face.
Believe in what you see if it sees you back.

The more than relative and the less and lesser relative zero in on absolute between.
The multiple values in displaced agency are.
Gather up all the meanings a word can hold releasing willingly to the currents.

The unexpected transparency of dense language realizes on the spot.
I imagine a light shining from behind the letters but I'm not seeing it.
Light for ears appears amplitudinously otherwise.

Value verbs by their nature.
The action is where you're not looking but *it* is, configuratively speaking.
Maybe I'm saying too much to be as lesser as it likes.

My heels turn under me as a final support incarnate.
I understand what I like, not what not or what likes me.
When it comes to life there's no comparison.

Sometimes you have to jiggle the handle to stop the flow.
Since Noah we know to avert the flood modality to awaken selectively.
If we drop the line of succession we have to wait for the next bus back.

What's the verb but the word that verbs?
Learn your language and then mine or vice versa, same difference.
Reach across the lull to touch the sound world saying, *don't turn back, turn out.*

O to be anonymous and famous in the same key, nay, ontononymous.
Saying handle is not the level saying handles as the level rises.
I write in this language where it's easier to write without style.

More biblical reference calls for more biblical knowing but the words won't name.
Lingual thinking further fractalizes nature fabric.
I'm reading you today's weather outcast.

It's time to celebrate middle action verbs.
Lift your glasses two handed from all three eyes and think it up.
Failed reference preserves absent pleasures.

Fear trivial fear.
Take refuge at the swivel point.
The mind is not turning around but finding its rounding turning.

Every title tells all within focus and that's everywhere unmooring.
You haven't lived until changing horses midstream.
Thinking gets away from us in the currents.

It's harder and harder to lie different.
Change druthers mid seme.
I've been waved.

Now there's all manner of ject.
All words consulted are subject pronouns on their trails.
Hypercorrection regrammatizes getting us drunkdriving saying the simplest things.
Never no measure.

Humble countenance merely facing facts.
                                              Charlie Chan

Eat it up eat it down wear a crown and no frown.
Seeking meaning in life blocks life.

Rhythm cracks like its voice pubescent.
Even a snail has momentum.

This gets slower and slower ahead of itself.
Getting back down to self-study of the alternative self of the moment.

Self is the sound of breast beating of varying intensity.
Thank you for letting me get that crown frown matter out of my system.

Self compounds self-compound selves.
Looking for meaning distracts.

I only have sidelines.
I'm being raptized.

Listen softly for the spiral behind all this.
Waving unseen is not *to* us but *through* us.

The looming judgment of the world the poem itself ignores.
What does it mean distracts?

Bad question to get some -jection sub specie initiatus.
We make things dumb dumbing things down.

A mode of denial courting both oblivion and ecstasy seeks protection unfamiliarly.

To operate magic is nothing other than to marry the world.
Pico della Mirandola, Thesis 9:13

A beautiful redhead shows through her wet gown so naked across the baptismal.
This is the raptized moment before self immersion.
I go in as me and come out as other.

Here we enter a low-pressure system of contrary belief.
I have to learn the faces of face-offs the heart generates.
Word masks.

Teasing out meaning forgetting she's a tease is believing in seduction.
Poetic mask is language laughing until it cries and vice versa verses.
Words matter that matter words.

It's about keeping the flow—intelligent.
Consider a dark magic of dates as if to typo a number drives time with whips.
Pen on paper scratches primordial time until it bleeds.

Commitment feels stronger in itself in the outfields of optionality.
People high the world over are street-cleaning the noesphere.
Verses versus furrowing toward.

So destabilized though small in scope makes for a kind of sunny insanity.
A truth knows its name thanks to its contrary.
Why do amazed disparate elements keep falling into place from linked blowholes?

I found the register to say *I am* not meaning me—not just now.
Being is the mantra voicing itself at zero.
Who is it I'm following at the end of the nose at the end of the line...

All processes in nature are interrelated;
and thus there could be no complete sentence...
save one which it would take all time to pronounce.
Fenollosa

Nonce precision.
No matter how you say it it's the same itself the same as nothing.
No once in the word is none other now as never.

All the words in a sentence modify each other as a matter of basic courtesy.
Intelligence may be everywhere but you can't get your finger in it till it says so.
A tongue does not extend beyond all its people.

Nonce is the one then.
It makes no sense otherwise, emphasis on other.
We seem to be being tested as to how we're handling not understanding.

Consent is all she wrote.
Reports are aiming at a moving center that has been hoarding intelligence.
Time to squeeze the space from the ears in.

The more you know the more you're unknown.
There's an outside chance she's hearing you as the windows are going both ways.
The object is referred to perfectly without your knowing.

Rhythms layer.
Hide inside long enough that being right here vows to keep.
Crossing includes crossing out.

No win wins all in all.
The permeable self benefits quietly from bad weather.

shadowing ideas
in the rearview mirror

permeable self benefits noisily from hard weather

Reading signs is in the foreground where the ground is doing the telling.

I'd never recognize myself if I didn't do this, though I don't recognize myself doing it.
It's only a problem when I meet myself in a dark alley of phantasy.
Recognition doesn't always meet the qualification of fact.

To say a thing truly the effect follows pervasive.
The subject follows itself absent.
I'm no follower knowing everything is on your tail trailing.

The work doesn't claim me the maker.

Taking credit is an anti-magical technique.
A sentence is a micro-ecosystem whose members have found their own way in.
I surject at points of recognition amidst alien species.

I know they're near when I fear my own.
Propriety avoidance is called for here—look female for the split instant, look up.
Attraction tracks through her trove of tricks.

Language thrives where hearing a beautiful woman has entered the room changes.

Turning around touches where time isn't.
Rhythm is your hand going in where you surround.

A sentence deepens according to who passes through crossing over yet returning.
The fell off back there in the feel of entitled.
Clarity the first time through is a dead end.

Music happens when following you slide between objects still unidentified.
So saying magic carpet is letteristic distortion with torsion and lift.

I'm experiencing the kind of curves that keep straight talk going off the road.
Words have corners to give us turning options without telos.

Continuing travelers belong to a club that never recognizes its members.
Upset set theory.

The unit cannot count on bounding.
And yet it keeps its bounce.

I'm not authorized to say this.
Belief is paradox with lipstick.

A couplet is where you lose count after two.
Poetry offers artificial support for rudderless reading with strong grounds.

Rhythm is a pulse with tailwind.
Its strength is the handsfree tone of willing speech.

Raga speaks with the other voice.
The long inhale holds the tongue on top.

Couple is something you do. Sometwo.
Words feel the join. Persons too.

Free of reliable fit oneself is free of proving self. Just one.

As a matter of principle, we cannot ever
exactly recognize the present.
W. Heisenberg

Precious meaningful leanings have been sneaking up on me again.
I'm crossing my fingers as an act of pure finding.
Allow me to point you toward what I still can't think.

Not saying eternal things speaks eternity the impossible way.
Poem is what is retained in the passthrough of particular propulsive words.
There's never no flow, like sacred seepage, evidence of timely loss.

The performance is performative of its own moment like getting out of bed.
The example is the meaning. The removal.

The motive is extracting oneself from danger as if weaving.
Getting off track is a curve surviving.
This has spot-intensive provenance meaning a thing here finds its spot on the porch.

Stripped of intention the line is free intending.
Things arrange themselves mainly behind your back so you may as well look up.
There can be no end to poetry because there can be no end to others.

Feeling plants, winter knows, not every logic finds its wise.
Time no longer flies, it jets by mind.
Irrational guilt about enjoying warm winter precedes the issue and knows no name.

Identity is what is retained in the passthrough of particular propulsive selves.
Just when I really have nothing left to say speaking takes over.
How can you say no when the grip feels like hers from the belly out.

What keeps a god hungry?
Paradise grows restless in retrospect.
Feeling it wants to know me brings me to the poem still willing.

Think Johnny Appleseed to grow diverse.
Disexpectation is hard to integrate with dining, likewise reading without comfort.
Identity won't lie still.

Every apple a tower of Babel.
Things know their fate by the end user.
Diffuse to choose.

Paradisal restlessness may mean don't look back. Ambivalent I/O.
Refuse to prove.
It strikes like lightning or not at all but a single firefly will do.

I'm forever shadowing ideas in the rearview mirror.
The past never stops moving forward however stalled here in hot pursuit.
If Martians still talked like Jack playing house might risk a right idea about love.

There's never no meaning.

Some things come through pre-torqued like desire.
Some one shows through like tears in the fire.
Tares, tiers, you hear your spot when *it* hears *you*.

Rejections, reflections, connections sound different and the same just this once.
Listening slants accordingly.

Poetic distance is risky.
Identity still lies.
We're learning to wait faster.

There's a halftime show somewhere in every contending sentence.
Grammar the language deterrent and poetic flame retardant cages until loosed.
The cipher is the sequence.

The wild shows in angled mirroring neuronic syntactics alone.

These opinions belong to no one. They are free agents.
No one has birthright to invariable interpretation.
Judgments are incursions that feel like mirrors.

Referring to your ideology to know what to say is to forget how to speak.
Survey is a reflex of acquired artificial intelligence.

Infinity in word gaps and possible between welling is nature's sway hypnotic.
Incredibly you can dance to it, and it helps overcome the burden of looking good.
There's a corner open to any truth told in its own rhythm.

Syntactic parallax is rarely taken into (reading) account at the operative angles.
It's like keeping track of the operative angels referentially dispossessed.
Displaced reference and slight of particle impair presumed dignity of subject.

Obstructed reading grieves for loss of preferred perspective.
Sovereign dignity is always at risk.
The merry-go-round stills while the world talks in circles.

By which may one be said to embrace the moment as atemporal fate.
Beside this the tangle of belief is a massive believing mess.

The warrior poet drinks smoky mescal on the other side of liking.
Proof of daimon is the energy from nowhere.

The post-poetic as *God is dead* is no less than writing finding out *it's here*.
Certain of my ideas have not weathered well in this climate.

Variable thoughts catch like bramble—can't go forward, can't go back.
They're thingly like thrown emotional thistle and you're the target.

A do-nothing god were the source of new being thinking saying.
Not controlling things you get to witness unexampled witchery self-reconnoitering.

Like not like flick flack.
This is the sound from down under up up and away.

You're helping me track these geophysical belief currents. Read on.
Reading is not ending with the line.

Poetry is a headcleaner.
So the tape can play out—going all the way.

Check the belief report because it's weather.
In my crystal peak dream brittle faced off on glisten in building this cabin outpost.

For the neverbefore said the time has come to let time go and dwell between lines.

Assignment: Ask a question showing neither existence nor non-existence.
Now we can take our lunch break on Mt. Etna as fleas on a bull, tail still swishing.
Between beats there's a ping you're not sure you heard in time.

You can't both permit her to speak freely and demean her message of no message.
Her, or if you prefer, *it*'s no object to your subject messaging.
We fall into place as she goes, my captain, this wavy imbrication notwithstanding.

Failing to master the system I walk freely within it.
Learning to take running thought in stride, for the boost.
Meaning here is by flicker (*seizure warning in effect*).

We weather the weather with beliefs full flagrante.

Releasing multiple selves is an anti-repressive technique homegrown.
They're waiting for a mathematics of ego-crowding for all the good it will do.

The poem builds like a sand pile, no foretelling the avalanche.
Heavyhanded ego-busting may be dangerous to your health as well as bystanders.
Self-splitting escapes oppression even while releasing the inward hiding slaves.

Disaster is perspectival, gifting stars not included.

All bite and no bark, no flight and all work.
In poetry your inner crazies are talking to themselves without coercion.
Visionary conceptualism spells trouble on the plane of reading for sake of rescue.

Ruining thought loving thinking does.

Collective hypnosis is the way weather surrounds us together.
I only follow the ramifications that bounce off your skin.
Why does it take so long to get here?

No secrets are safe here so be sure to tell nothing.
That you can't help living permanence style is stepping on your own toes.
Notwithstanding unconscious intricate organization willing to show.

Secrets only pretending to seek safety is the secret itself.
Fingers trip over letters to take us in between.
The never thought is a haven.

Here the blemish is beyond itself in the clear.
Self tripping is the dance afoot.
Just as my fingers on these keys shake music down.

The dying fall-off.
Cliffs and arrows of desire, interpersonal fire.
Knowing the mind goes further off.

This thought is the water the dog shakes off.
The honey trap shelters the syntactic flap.
I look like I'm napping but I call it meditating, calling from afar without leaving.

Godly says things power up being being things think godly for power.
Playing with knives slackrope walking over our own canyon don't look down.

We're here together to think out of a need for music.

Think beast.
Making music out of a need for the wild like leaping salmon.
Empty plate is a core attractor.

A title is what has consequences long after.
The poem is learning to live with not seeing it coming.
I am intimate in mind with adversaries improving my dance shooting at my feet.

Looking for my lost verbs every word began to move and some went dangling.
Dinner plate, name plate, gold plate template, contemplate.
Things long to be called into question.

It's difficult to believe in reality.

Folding money, folding memory, folding laundry, folding tunes turning back in.
Water over the bridge, as my mother used to say, reflecting a life.
Art is seeing what you see seeing what she sees.

The poem is mystified when a person pays it close attention.
Why do you knock on my door?
Before I caught the wave I was outside looking in on you.

Suddenly I know who I am I say to myself with mirrors.

Names saying things power up being being things thinking names for power.
Signification is caught in an updraft of turned-on word tension.
We're walking along on a hot night lake shore with breeze voicing.
Just dropping names along the way.

Fanning imprisoned stroke thrusts back the horizon delicately.
Air erotics in closure exposes.

Leaping salmon have a math that to say is to know the poetics you don't.
Face it says to you you're turning around saying *turn around.*
Water over the bridge is the view from the ridge.

The non-thinking is saying the laxing language is doing the thinking.
How many edges wedge in there to weigh, stray.
You drag your meaning over one ledge to another.

Why do I resist?
Poem stirs, reader stirs crazy.
A text all action is flex with reflexes.

The lightness is it levitates.
Odd music is the gods strange even to themselves.
You summon their difference, they mirror.

Listening to Ali's raga far enough in you find his Bach as you find your tongue.
To mime it you rime the time in.
Somewhere in here over there the point is the joint.

Music's cursive bounds.
Word tails tell from behind.
It does what it sounds to itself to get here.

Driving it down inflames.

Only free seeing discovers self secret relations lifting your eyes high.
Feeling the fruiting bodies has sublingual appeal.
There's perfection that can't appreciate itself.

Learning to speak an alternate language lets things intersect obversely.
This is about how we double back when nothing's there. *So* there.
I can't get my hands all the way around this empty, but it has feel.

You register the wave coming in the palm sounds.
This ends in nonsense sensed ever better.

The poem is entitled to its title.
It lives in the belly of its prediction.
Poem is consequence of title—playing down.

The minute musics between beat.
There's no telling *when* when *when* tells.
This is a soundscape landing where you walk your talk without a lead.

It muscles underfoot.
You get so close to the syllable you feel the ripples enclosing.
You've never been there nor will you ever though you are.

Self-true sounds grate on you.
Climbing over from behind mounts the fountain in the sound, *It joy'd.*
Feeling qualifies the way in.

Calling a music breaking out within an endless middle unbounds an expanse.

Writing is friction first.
Breathing speaks that grates on the tongue.
According aspiration is something less and greater than gourmet cannibalism.

It is vital to extend our reach to include transtending relations.

All words are invented to be reinvented like volcanic slopes.
Heat, myth of a god forging inside, eruptive passionate driving out and up, spoken.
Only free reading discovers self secret relations under threat of banishment.

Tame the inner fascist fundamentalist freak loudly drowning out poem sense.
Why do I have to wear myself down to a paper thin fade to pick up these signals?
Healing noise tells a tale on you.

The poem relieves you of the burden of the unthinkable by living impossible mind.
Help wanted holding the spaces safe. Species saved.
Memory is in peril.

The sign is we're disappearing discovering what appearance is.
Once I could remember what I was going to say before I knew.
The truth is not an instant before.

Conscience is a two-edge sword, one cutting through the present with a vengeance.
Feeling for the other in the dark comes with risk.
Memory is a peril.

Makes me feel so oral to title birthing.
Linguality's mission's making belief in it next to impossible.

Self true sounds irritate the sense of recognition.

What makes me me? is never told.

No point saying you *are* when change is quicker than the I.

Lines expect nothing of you, feared reader.

Poem says get close but not too close.

Just trying to keep the phonemic bounds in this echoing canyon.

Calling into question has a sexual side.

The mirror says I'll be reborn as the volcano I resist.

Neurons rime among morons too.

Naming has consequences.

A title is to be grasped between the teeth.

Birth, love, language, death, eating, sleeping, writing, own logic.

This is thought at 2:22 PM EST on 2-22-16.

Everything symbolizes when you let it.

The what is not to say what.

A rhythm of thinking accords to the potholes walking.

Everything dangles from some angle. Like angels syntactic.

Making nothing new you are new.

Correcting the poem corrects my self.

Maturing cuts down on thinking what you're doing.

Save the thought before it self obliterates.

The endless poem is a feeling of living forever right now.
The flexing sound calls home to the center it never left.
Welcome to angular space aloft in your own canyon.

Life shows up as open total.
There are laws that law knows not.
Call it paradox but there's unknown orthos with own dox.

It's music when the phonemic boundaries come into play.
Syllables up close feel the nipples exposing.
Intertextual is intrasexual.

The lingual overflows of mind knowing itself is an other poetry.
There's perfection with no outside.
Problems transtend to be intergenderational.

Not only by association but unannounced attractors things incur to mind.
Hail mongrel in this site of unforeseeable hybrids.
Daimon is the pressing in indefatigably.

You can't like everything because there's no everything to like.
Suspend knowing where you are. Now who. Now how.
Showing invents.

Mind has its reason that reason knows not.
Gently restraining any symbolizing predisposition allows for companion gendering.
Almost writing my name as the place name tells me grounding absorbs to feed roots.
Body is ear.

Life forgets it's raw.

Obviously language rebels against saying only what I mean.
I'm finding not knowing what I mean is everywhere perceptibly.
Just noticing it I'm too tired not to be ecstatic.

Never give up merely because the situation is hopeless, says the empty hand.
It's nothing new under the sun given that everything is newly unnoticed nightly.
Showing invents the inventor.

A theme is what can't stop showing up.
There's always room for untold slogans.
Be here not only.

Perceptual separation leading to spirited embrace is ironically joined here now.
It's the way we play in our sandbox so to speak from birth on earth.
Accurate inner swirl minimalizes thinking in the instant.

We need to evolve beyond punch lines.
Clichés are bad for your teeth.
Poem entrains body. Emphasis on tongue.

Index fingers the pen to know it in writing.
Gathering a live tradition from the water proves deep sea diving therapeutics.
Poem is body part and don't ask which.

In dream the self peeling fruit gave herself to the mouth agreeing with itself.
That would be preposterous if the vivid attraction stopped there.

ȝeve þi cunte to cunning / and crave affetir wedding
Give your cunt with cunning / And demand after wedding.
Hendyng's Proverb [c.1325]

Writing is blessing flagrante in the emptiness of page.

The poem with no symbols symbolizes promiscuously.
Symbol is the mark of distinction for the word slipping free quicker than *I* sees.
By the same token the empty allegory pretends nothing beyond its right to be.

Symbol is the same thrown wider yet.
A watch word discovers self-watching at your expense.
Get out your double cast net amphiboly and let's go fishing.

A statement is evading its own question. You feel it before it does.

Are there symbols that practice telekinesis?
What about that one that gets you hot?
It's redefining itself in the mind as we speak, way above our heads.

I almost understand what I say it says I say and hope to yet.
To revisit the past is to follow the leaks and we end up here reading the signs.
When you get right down to it poetry is spooky. Part of a greater ooze.

To mistake non-resolution for non-meaning is to miss how what we mean means.
Liberation of inner symbolotrous slaves is a lost priority.
Lament for the lost self-validating enwrapping monosyllable begins now.

Anything can come into it but nothing is necessary to it.
The act of its happening in your action draws out authoring between lines.
Under the waking fig under the woken fig tree.

190

I walk through your life with mirrors on my body.
Ignorance flows with an excitatory slivered lining.
Now back to the blank you thought was sleep.

In waiting the real punch never finds its line.
Just because you think you've heard it before doesn't make it a cliché unless you do.
It sounds clever until you learn its language and lose the meaning in the gamble.

Unthinking to rethink.
Attending the underflow requires a certain hang gliding faith.
You hear the guitar with solar plexus.

Words confess in the gut.
Ideas have texture and feel.
Thought smells.

The string strums in the bone.
You take in the self-kept secret of own self-manifestation.
Knowing your music knows you're music.

Freedom reduction by interpretation is not death by hanging except the construct.
Similitudinously conservation does not conserve to keep living. Living conserves.
The technique of appropriation applies to the noesphere without claiming territory.

The middle voice reflex can only tell you itself.
Symbolizing it retains power remaining unknown vividly.
You can use it solely if you find your lack.

Life chances you take your chances to heart.
The surge feels behind even when I know to say around.
There's no piling in balancing.

Speaking on the fly still steering life at hand through unanticipated sense currents.

Symbol prick bleeds displaced desire.
The inactive reflex is reflexive.

Symbol masks what it exposes.
Camouflage effects safe blending.
Would it were ever other than apathetic verbal simulacra ringing your church bells.

False can save.

You discover the chance operations are intentional when it dawns on you.
Look up the word excites.
You're seeing her as your sky writing.

Streaming leads strand in flight.
Shut up it's love poetics caving in under fleshed out flashing in the dark.
Blazing blazons do not saddle mind with meaning for long.

Conjunctive irony causes conceptual separation leading to spirited embrace.
The symbol is displaced concreteness.
The strange one is an edge reflex.

It's one thing to theorize a field and the other is to sail your boat back through.

Life scares.
It's a core tactic.

I lost the thread years ago standing up for my stranded human.
Strategically forgetting oneself turns to self remembering following a filament.

There is a necessary fright in our trafficking in the unthinkable.
Me I'm just loitering among my lacks looking for new growth.

Of course the meaning field isn't really there but let's say it is.
It's good for seeing through. Saying through.

Further steering the life at hand on through unforesees multiplying currents.
Hold on to your cat.

You don't know which side you're on.
I'm just being Schrödinger's brat.

Meaning comes ruthlessly independent of me showing me independent of myself.
Any order you find here is true enough to write home about but don't ask me.

Learning from your mistakes is overrated! The contrary even more so, and different.
Life beginning to wear you down masks your letting go.

The bigger the ordeal the sweeter the release it affords.
Wrong is not right now.

No need to dwell long to dwell right.

What I say to you is never what I say to you
but something else instead.
Clarice Lispector

Concealing the truth from you begins in the throat—I swallow it back.
This is not no doubling negation—maybe tripling, maybe tripping.

We're not just getting by here.
The enfolding concealing throat chokes on truth.

You won't like what I'm going to say just like me.
The textured surface figures.

Liking doesn't cut it.
Life is looking over my shoulder to see itself in my mirror.

Self-seeing distorts by seeing seeing.
The no-goal goal is the goal of goals.

Repetitive thought is the illusion that we are not on the edge and part way over.
Poetry is non-resignation to the stunning force of ordinary language.

Making things new is more leaving them alone than doing anything to them.
Any lingual disassembling of the stun gun of common speech has some poetic force.

There is no non-contradiction for more than a moment.
Soon we may see why endlessness is inevitable.

The line needs no time to register its quest in question.
Laughing listens with the whole body.
There are voices in the strings.

Writing is for the willing either living or dead.
The wildness of her poet mind variably measures the tessitura of its line unfolding.
The same seems to look for its answers to the question still not asked.

Loving words is taking the blows with grace reaching into the dark places.
Saying *I* as self circling in itself is an esoteric meaning of *esoteric*.
Self-obscurity is endemic to waking.

A self-true line is thrown from the navel.
Naming gestures before it tells.
Implicit identity never quite gets out.

I write from the grave that is already beyond itself.
"*I identify with the impersona*" corrupts both personal and impersonal faithfully.
Writing is how you happen to yourself from outside.

Identity fears exposure.
To find your question backdates the inquiry to the actual start, too fragile to focus.
The line signs as the mind dines.

Writing has register that calls to you from your own grave not here, always here.
Renunciation is superfluous seeing life closely delivering itself of all but the platter.
Celebrate the space you are slowly vacating.

No expectation the bright thought will serve the next so-called moment.
This all but proves the need for poetry, the visioning rescue vehicle—but whose?

Identity is a disguise.

I overheard you bleeding when suddenly you flew the dream.
Some discover another stream thinking itself otherwise.

Anything meaningfully said is thrown from its possessor like a rider.
The riding writing happens extramindedly.

Gender is a disguise.
Everything said is secret before its moment.

When all is said and done all said and done lingually is doublespeak, with accent.
What if everything said had the exclamation point it desires!

I didn't like the smoky mescal but drank it daily until it opened a door to my earth!!!
The logic of a snapshot—that is, logic—has the authority of a glimpse, tiny aperture.

Deep disguise rarely comes off.
The desire to please melts in time if left out of the freezer.

Life is extended denial.
Death is the built in life scandal no prowess handles.

Ecstasy is pain that no longer knows its name or even itself nameless.
Reading writing reading revives displaced mind through filaments past body life.
You say a thing you don't know so someone else can imagine it back for you.

Any thought thought here lengthens by retention.
Leave it alone for once.
Otherwise the thought hemorrhages.

The virtues of avoiding thinking straight are underplayed.
Things issue their hidden beauty in raw relations beyond comparison.
And now for the questions that befuddle and do not need to be asked.

Sorry, there's interference on the ancient line, no more questions tonight.
Instead the true text surrenders to melodic contour unexpectingly.
What is wisdom asks itself in the structure of inquisitorial linguality, no answer.

The disease of comparison is the inevitable result of self preservation.
More factors activate within a statement than the statement itself tracks.
When all is said and done next to nothing has been said or done. Onward.

An explanation point would out the straight-faced exclamation the mind won't face.
The true text you read so you can't say what you read.

If the line speaks, it's poetry; if it shows, it's drawing.
The true text has no memory and therefore never repeats itself.

Awareness is the opening trap staying open.
The true text feels you losing your mind and comes to the rescue unrequested.

Real teaching is self-teaching.
The true text experiences blind faith in you in the purposeful absence of belief.

The only reading that lets you into its writing is an act of obedience to unknowns.
There is scarcely a true text, which fact conceives scarcity for the better.

If I say this is now I betray reality in the way it requires for non-being to be.

Time starts now.
There was no time beforehand.

Life's not awaiting your completion but for you to grasp its desiring incompletion.
How many nows make a right now?

Talking books you read it but it never gets read.
It remains gender fluctuant.
Being bi is bio. Challenging thought.

If we say the future has arrived we demonstrate how stupid time is.
Writing opens the way to living the moment knowing it's its.
You read into incompletion.

The clock is retreating to higher ground.
Maybe now we can peacefully live in ignorance.
The book like me is equal parts rotting humus and new growth.

The future is life getting ahead of itself—bad habit.
I'm rushing into stillness, I'm not here yet.
There are books you never read but read you by night until you wake.

More addiction to self importance, eh, Don Juan?
Some things are only understood by way of bone.

Let's believe in secret masters pushing through the crowd to grip the impersona.
You are your face not in the way you think but as you are thought, she says.
Actual thinking shakes you down.

The poem speaks the language I am about to learn.
Reading it back completes the teaching I barely perceive. Thank you, I think.

If the poem isn't pushing you back it isn't liking you.
If you fit too well in your skin you may drift normal.
Distraction from distraction is an esoteric hard line.

My senses are letting the world know itself.
Poetry is a name for doing its talking.
On the other hand the poem is the sole oracle of life from its other side.

Evolution may be moving toward metaphors with no comparative starting point.
A pure leap of being requires no verb.
Just as the piano is born of Beethoven's need.

I could say the need here is everything playing on the sarode and I could faint.

Freedom is the carrying out of any gesture intended in startling awake.
Radical reading is a field of urged thinking.
There are familiar voices in the cords catching on words.

I'm speaking to you through my organ of sensation.
Now it's paper and flesh and then it's the idea of paper and flesh.
Skin fit is a waking achievement.

Who can accept verbal non-sequence as configurative integrity equal to personal?
Just as banging *on* is drumming response to need to be without starting point.
Each word the omen of a life, just as.

Having something to say is a blinding force.
From childhood I felt cheated by fakes because I want to believe in everything.
I go blind nightly from knowing too true.

The confusion of beginnings shows loving most intense in dark places.
Eternal return is the again of never again.

The poem shows a passion I can't claim but study amazed.
Loving intensifies the dark until it shines.
Likewise creation divines parody of itself.

We live with others like supporting roles in our play, coming on and off stage.

Making love with great dead spirit is not necrophilia but life partnering obscurity.
Dying denies itself until it can't.
Time to give up the represented authentic.

I'm avoiding the satisfaction of mastering ideas.
What am I saying? I can't say.
In the beginning God made simulacra the order of the day.

Inside linguality nothing unsayable remains.
Impermanence protects us against the same.
This line gathers faith cognitive vertigo prefigures further equilibration.

According to certain ETs without hilaritas humanitas is not.
They say the eternal same of perpetual difference is.
I ask the world's forgiveness that my trance of birthing excludes so much of it.

Openness is scale-invariant.
Lone is the loving one.
Bespeaking healing glyphs.

Language has mystery coming from unexperienced sides.
Just as instruments are insights into what music didn't know it was they say.
What does it feel like it's saying that it can't not be saying also.

Come closer so I can tell you in cheiroglyphs.
Meaning is instrumental to the state longed into.

Poetry changes the world where you're not looking.

Close reading is hands-on.
You know the text is hyperventilating when it makes you dizzy.

Humans are entities subject to self-organized fuck-up with mysterious criticality.
It burns me up to think this way.
The more certain you are the more fragile the truth disguised.

What once you think truly can't not be true?
No argument covers it.
The most intense words refer to what isn't yet there.

I am my disguise but I wasn't a moment ago.
If you still know who you are the poem is failing.
The mood changes before the line ends proves true once again as never before.

A poem can't end until it knows what it came for you came for.
This is called reverse reading.

It ruses with reason.
Dissembled identity animalizes (verbs intransitive).

I become myself through my disguises and I'm more than happy to be here.
Every leap goes crazy midair.

Singular action must remain vigilant for the men in white coats.
Commonality surrounds with undetectable force.

You think you just heard a word you didn't proves lingual entanglement.
We're reading our way through a field of resistance but is it working?

Some kinds of excitement block ecstasy by preconditioning the space, closing doors.
Whereas poetry is the art form of reading between time and no time.

Constants are perspectival and scale-dependent.
Avoiding repetition means recognizing there isn't any.

Driving through lingual mountains quick glimpsing protopreverbs flashing blind.
You can't put the same foot in your mouth twice.

A word is the end point of a gesture of mind that sometimes misses the mark.
I never forget the sound of words droning over the abyss.

The lingual silver lining is a carpet said to fly.

We tend what we see.
I'm looking after my words, it's the mother in me.

I repent the demolished anthills of childhood now offering restoration.
You nurture what you fail to condemn.

Start up in the continuous crisis of being in the body.
A faithful leap is the work of canyon lubbers.

Words excite when excited in a way unforeseen.
I'm being read to from the unknowable, it must be her.
I hide to trick my nature into thinking it's safe to appear.

Flipping through the book I got the message I missed reading.
Soulworked reading happens deep into the line for its inflorescence.

The habit of continuity is anti-ecstatic.
You name what you think you know.

She the woman reading up from the page is scaled to orchid as born again art.

No need to follow along as I repair the world in retrospect.
This is happening down the serpent hole.

Death is life in its darkest disguise.
Time to apologize for self-damage on a global scale.

The carpet flies because you look at it right.

We're here to set back the agenda.

The scribbled line is all along lingual action.

Reading own poems is narcissism interruptus.

Hardwired to *prefer* doesn't stop stepping back into field mind free moving center.

Just saying that makes me thirstily seek the inmost indeterminate infructescence.

The syntactic mantra is *soft belly*.

We tame what we name but it may not last.

What plants make me say like books making me array.

Meditation is feel-good for the unknown.

The day field is the atmosphere of the poem, while moonstruck.

Drawing fragments into their desiring arrangement is a poetic by unfollowing.

I read these lines as a diary found in another time. Gender indifferent.

The text speaks to prepare me to speak but it won't stick.

An actual thought is what has never been thought before.

Grasping thinking is willing the surprise in its instant.

Earth touching gesture: own pulse relinquishes in infinitely slower flow-pulsing.

I'm all the race horses in my life never finishing.

Music is the pulse made audible.

There's a stillness that haunts excitement down to the toe tips.

Listening happens right up to the edges of mind.

Enlightened mind doesn't care about you.

Names make days differ.
One means what it says even as I wobble in conviction.

I love Sunday.
Monday worries.
Tuesday wars.
Wednesday snakes.
Thursday thunders.
Friday frees.
Saturday saturates surround.

Now we are free for Friday to start the tense release.
Just passing through the name I'm lighter.
Thirsty on Thursday expands lately.

The same inflames. Conjunctive ironitis.
Self-remembering is reflexive and not.
Waking life outfoxes itself to evade its addiction to entrapment.

Tantric buggery does not pick sides.
Gender sections off sexual insignia.
The poem with no symbols symbolizes with shameless abandon.

All things being equal which they never are this is all doubly true.
The mind is a liar and its pants are on fire and nothing left but aspire.
We're going forward with unplanning the high pleasures of uncertainty.

Amphiboly is the two-way narrow alley making itself yours in a flare-up.

Today is a near-life experience.
Being deadly serious beneath my ridicule requires drawing back the cover story.

Interior fear huddles.
Resistance contraction is hugging your body from within.

Holding on too long loses the guts.
I don't deny the dark moods blowing across the icy lakelike surface mirror.

Saying so chastens in hot contact on a cold bed.
It keeps me when I loosen the grip on me.

Originality is where the contact point is unaccountable.
You know it's itself when it hasn't thrown you off its back.

I'm looking into language that talks to the you you never met.
So many have gone dark we can't shake knowing the other side denying what is.

The mind blinks life gone.
Nothing new always new.

I confess confession calls cold.
It's true setting you free on the wild seas in a sieve.

Tomorrow is getting ahead of itself.
The watcher is looking itself in the eye. No blinks.

Darkly speaking it sits on the mind like the self-lit fog it isn't.

It starts when you feel the speaking free itself inside from the gut.

The truth is here to betray itself before slipping away.
I'll take responsibility for your incoherence if you'll compossibilize mine.

The level of lining attracts the words.
We're in the middle of a storm here as viewed in our movie, the swirl.
If the poem didn't know more than I do I would have figured it out by now.

I'm reporting back to the you I don't know.
I'm bee watching to find the intricate flight path in returning.
It requires tuning in to the ready to tune.

Birds symbolize on the fly.
Before I die I aim to talk through everything.
Do I repeat myself, no.

Living pulse is constant in its inconstant same.
A word is an entity capable of avoiding the same meaning twice.
Part of me knows what it's saying but not this part.

Symbols go bad when you try to stabilize them.
Thought rushing ahead of its saying loses its grip.
Longing goes longer.

Left listening to the edges of the mind barely making use of my pronoun.

Without seeing squarely whatever comes I don't know why I'm alive.
Teaching is talking to one's other self.

Impersonation is the wagons circling without you.
Study the grip. Even when you can't see what's held.

Everything has a curve and thrown it's parabolic.
I'm here giving poem-mind a poet to play on.

This has been a long rhythm hanging in with lax ways.
There's a parable about the tastelessness of taste ripening but no one recalls it.

A true statement leaves room for its contrary.

I know I'm still talking with it when it's still talking with me.
I willingly live the instrumental with.

The parable in the parabola has a running start with millennia of meaning.
Momentum can't shake the hold of its feel.

If there's a point it's getting the mojo out of the *like this, don't like that* traps
Act while it feels there.

Fresh simulacra have their own ungraspable self sameness.
Writing knowing it's real acts the emissary into the fog of others.

Birth questions in flesh. Happens all the time.
You learn to stand still listening when you know you are born that way.

not even rabbits go down this hole

for Jerome McGann

I refuse to die until I've been fully born.
I don't know the secrets but I feel them moving around inside.
Perhaps the accurate feel is the life escape or slip into where life is outside itself.

Ear to the rim hears you say the beautiful thing guaranteed to hurt my ordinary.
Slanderous secrets are not secrets.
Romantic insights embarrass when too true.

Secrets are what have successfully avoided the maps.
It's time for eye to page resuscitation.
Turning page turning mind.

Marked time passes fast differently.
Runaway mind drops its bridle.

Dying will have nothing to do with the word—the right ones come in their no time.
Happiness hurts waning.
Being right is tedium out of its cage.

The secret radiance you see is an act of self protection.
Like language it makes no promise to communicate.
You can't place its rhetoric or hold on to an eel.

It's natural like reader pressing poet to say what she doesn't understand.
The answer is no.
The sorcerer sings out of tune to an end.

The end should be flamenco with sudden flare unbearably beautiful, so no end here.

I'm feeling a delectable uselessness.
The real *this life* is barely a scent.

The thought trailed off before it got to me.
This is my net for carefully dropped ecstasies.

Life no longer wants me walking too far from here.
I'm tethered by attention I scarcely have.

Looking out on here things are more detached than they look.
I'm still hunting down the radio with scar tissue, Orpheus.
Honor the stain defining the way roundabout through.

If you're feeling safe you haven't arrived at this spot moving sideways downwards.
Watch for the hole even rabbits won't go down.

Dreaming awake slackropes writing.
This is just another cave outside timespace.

Bad to push symbols which push back in turn.

A line is an act wanting me different.
I have to let the words dry out before using so as to sniff out fresh cracks.

Landscape is a site of things secretly connected in their escape from view.
This is what I could think right here, and the wind blows through me.
I can barely recall this moment.

Rumoring jungle insects invented the bamboo flute so the wind could play human.
This is the stuff of myth which is the stuff of intolerable focus.
It's real when there's no guarantee. *Duende!*

Slackrope writing is an open imperative.
Lines wave across the page in an effort to completely be upright.
Miraculous verticality is a horizontal dream writing all out.

If you see the line activity from above notice the hieroglyphic movement freestyle.

Certain books avoid understanding reading cultivating theretofore impossible flight.
Mind takes off midsentence. *Querencia!*
Accuracy differs from itself shot by shot.

Stumblebum thinking has its own yoga.
No taking aim like butterflies.
Two wings required for the single thought.

It's gone, it's coming, it's anywhere that's here. I'm thinking *music.*

Where thinking lies the heart lies.
Dying starts long before when old friends drift to the silent margins.
A complete poetry completes the life as complete teaching.

There's no wiggle room without a body.
Line by line it adjusts its sightings on me. Hello Lake!
Nothing's the same but I live it the same.

Music delays the inevitable indefinitely in the moment.
Sad song makes a rail like a Braille for the limping mind.

Thinking torque says torsion thinks.
What does *one another* mean that's so instantly beyond otherness.

Relation reflexes.
The question mark is reserved.

Things senselessly said out of context expose the skeleton in the grammar.
Words hide from you their secret meaning to ensure reading incurs.

The fate of words is to intransitize.
Verbal sex change is a power reflex.

Every syllable wakes a consort suspensed between the ears.
Third versed hearing plays out the two.

Music peels away.
Footfalls actually listen.

The center gets physical with the incursions.
Numberless cabalas count in skin.

A thing's initials initialize you to initiate the next reading.
A reading is reading itself reading to itself. So I listen.

I become what I hold.

Today is the day that never happens again in my lifetime.
It's time for the alternative civilization building up all this time.
Actual intelligence is interlaced.

I have faith you are following my thought far better than I.
Poet is one willing to travel second class just to get to go along with the song.
Tone deaf until this moment.

It's hard to believe the world begins right there out front.
No one notices anarchists being born again by the moment.
Once you start you never stop aspiring to write with tasteless taste.

This is a pep talk to glide without hope of landing.

The poem I seek owns self-defeating as a path beyond the edge.
Landscape up close is capable of anything.
The map is its own territory and invites you eye first.

Its same taste is non-self-tasting.
Restless contentious is a path beyond dogma.
Looking closely the thing doubles at least.

Any moment is on the verge of knowing what no moment can know.
Some music returns to tell ancient history to the root.
It teases out the koans trailing under the lingual radar.

Reading own work as sacred proves it's not one's.
Proto music is older than old.

Today is the other day that never happens in my lifetime so how is it I know of it?
Learning own language badly is necessary to clue in, eh Detective?

In real prophecy prediction is neither here nor there.
The test of a saint is faith in understanding readers where language emerges free.
I carve away at the surface to find the syntax inside, running wild.

Language evolves by dangling.
Metaphors are dying to mix it up.

Linguality up close whispers what you'd just as soon not hear.
The self-sensible tongue teaches itself alien.
Close listening is a doubler.

Everything here chooses itself behind our back.

When you get hooked on the syntactic Doppler effect it's probably a poem.
A proleptic line knowing what it is before it begins is still forgetting by the end.
If you knew all this before you have existence to look forward to.

The ancient poem takes itself away in time to make space for meaning.
Soon come the modifiers hoping to dangle in plain sight.
No axes to grind yet growth axes extending subterranean indiscriminant mentalia.

Culture ignores the joy of having become oneself—the alien.
Dangling modifieds are primal deviants offering healing hope to metrophobia.
The writing hand is the nerve of this moment registering the start, day's startle.

Take me to the lost & found for suddenly fruiting verbal formulations vanished.

How to track the disappearing never before seen?

There are tones in the garden only green ears appear to hear.

Backroom speaking is keeping repeating what flares darker than dark.

In a set with smoky mezcal that must be drunk daily a door opens to your earth.

If it has the same taste it's tasteless.

Force of poetic environment drives the change in names on the land, listen round!

Metaphor is a lever of difference despite the comparative addiction.

The writing hand is not the upper hand.

Culture destabilizes owning.

The Golden Rule requires a *not* for masochists.

Metaphor is learning to leap over into the unspeakable gap.

It's difficult not to doubt a spirited thingness in the gut.

Fail good.

The odd sock is one thing that does find its way down the rabbit hole.

It's an odd thought and longs for the strange place that preserves it.

It feels in waiting for us.

Only negate with a stirring attitude.

The esoteric truth of the esoteric is that its truth is innate like fire.

Metaphor walks the plank over turbulence and never saves itself.

You are as able to fly right as you know you are born that way.

Some thinking is bottom up.
Managing chaos *is* not.

Listening improves when you think it's for you.
Taking myself seriously indicates taking myself ludicrously.

The sense of mission is uncovering before recovery.
Nonsense calls for an original dignity.

Danger thrills if for you death trills.
Whatever you're thinking about is more present than you are.

Art is tracking self unknowings.
And there's no way to know what that means one instant before it owns up.

Writing is listening when it gives up awareness of this fact.
There's a right moment for everything except this fact used as plan.

Listening is more mysterious than talking unless talking realizes it's listening.
Practice dulls.

They call it music, you hear music, then doubting it you doubt yourself.
Faith is for laughing better.

Listening re-experiences itself when it loses track of its object not losing intensity.
Time to imagine off-reading.
Conclusions are not drawn.
Not answering self chooses. No knee jerks.

We're taking a break from seduction for the current bardo.
Let the appetite rage to its heartless content.
Content talks back for no good reason.

If no narrative tells it true no story goes bad.
The words are angling for a better view.
They look for chances to get the mind off to the side.

The source can't be found but it's palpable.
It's subject to palpation in the cocked head position.
It speaks right past one's addiction.

It's uncomfortably unfamiliar like sleeping in a different bed every night.
A change of pace is neither good nor bad but it's felt in the gut.
Embodying at the charged angle is never convenient. Body up. Body out.

Reading in bed is bad if your angle is bad for the bed.
Sincerity is something you can never be sure is present.
An almost inaudible movingly real talk pulls at the strings you can't quite locate.

Confession is not true because of what it says.
Listening to what is there affirms being there at all.
Non-commitment to what is being heard may not be listening at all.

Confession tones true or not.
Metaphor learns when I speak through a wild cat's face.
I'm surprised to be here in any form.
Stay with it a line longer it stays with you.

Everything becomes more possible the word following.
The feel of the breeze syntactic modulates the body electric.
Her body shapes its way just seeing her saying her here.

It's that I can't tell you through the fog to know you from Eve.
Same difference is how we tell.
We can't tell our selves apart.

I don't believe in epistemology, she whispered, proving jokes mean what they say.
Drama comes into life where you pretend not to be looking.
A poem can't find where it's looking until you do.

The way it means itself is walking through your house not knowing it instantly.
The body alien territory lays me down to sleep. This is its map of no scare.
The bottom line shakes until moving along feels between its dopplers.

I can't help getting familiar evolving by attraction.
No place for minding is not an option.
Getting close to utterance muttering mothering closes in on her meaning.

You don't learn these ways.
People performing make me nervous if I forget I'm not them.
Then I'm them even with no them there.

Their education puts things in your way trying to lead you out.
No name in no time.
Personal irony is I don't only mean this.
I can make no claim to represent myself.

It feels like writing in circles but it's spheres and alleys with turnings.
I still don't understand language and yet I get you.

Nothing changes until one's appalled by what sticks to the mind in the me.
I claim I make no claim to having said the above. The me theme.

Why do anything?
The answer is instant by instant only if ever.

You say Samsara to remind yourself no matter how beautiful it is you're fucked up.
Elegance is nonsense of a higher order.

It's so music as a matter of posture movingly.
It teaches saying what makes me feel otherwise as myself.

Only at certain intersections is a thing's reading practicable.
Only taking what's handed over takes aim inadvertently.

Two times *only* splits the one direction, and we're off.
A line is an opportunity to be shone in the curve of oneself.

I get laid out as the posture of listening linearly radially.
It thinks in torcs visually historic to the seeing eye mood.

Disruptive artism teaches disruptive anticipation.
It puts things in your way to lead you out, said so.

It exposes itself with cave inspired vividness.

Far in toward the far end the dream gets realer than real.
You can't tell if you're either here nor there or neither either.
Real is your tongue twisting at cross purposes with what you think you're saying.

What saying you're doing is what I'm hearing the other way around.
This is the territorial hazard.
I'm here learning the reality of language to know the language of reality way around.

It's what you don't have to already know to know now.

There's echo, with no original.
A single string of cello raises up the body electric.
This discourse makes the cursive course.

Unforced lines of force do not force but allow release coherently bounding linear.
It seems to be happening but that's only one angle.
Being thinking is speaking true.

We think what we hear should excite like life which is never enough.
Could be.
Thinking gets urges.

Reading glimpses forces.
The lines haunt nature from within.
When music timely touches your timeless zone it stays near.

Not mine to reason sly but to shoo or fly.
She sings like this into my place of fear.

Sir, your persona is showing is the first line of the opera to come.
Such a tune carries involuntary satisfaction.

Thinking is only the never thought.
An instant thought is too quick to say like life.

I only like fantasy I can believe in once and for all; otherwise it's not fantastic.
The mirror spills.

I have nothing new to say this once only, which is why I'm trembling in the lip.
Sectioning the mirror only amplifies the same.

Multiplying the mask unmasks it.
To think this cuts in on identity.

We play this tune all night just to hear ourself think.
You can't focus on identity without slippage and danger to the body.

The blade is between the details or else the syllables.
The ear slices sounding finer than fine with me.

Meaning is that you don't know what it is but you know already.
Terminality runs alongside.

Language has tricks it never tells you for your own good.
It has no time to tell you how to read it yet it never stops telling.

Over time it cuts you through the veil until you know it's you.

Sir, your persona shows, middle voice.
Death is a character in my drama when it knows I'm not its enemy.

We co-star only but never can get it straight.
Life has my permission to think it's its own end.

I said it like a field for once just like the one it cannot not be.
The future human knows itself without bothering with these ideas.

Making impossible claims with a straight face is as utopian as it gets in these parts.
When I see 4s and 3s near each other I breathe in relief.

Lines rushing across pages are striving to stand up straighter than ever.
One another is a lot more than one other.

If we off-read long enough the latter-day logic will bleed through.
We know the world through self imposed stigmata.

By off-focus we discover ... but the thought trails off.
Thought interruptus leaves room for self outing desperate sublingual koans.

Life comes at all angles despite an aggressive preference toward direct-on.
You can't know what's the end in sight or when you enter ending.

The art carried all the way through is what no standard works for.
Music for my fears enclosing ears. It's all lettering.

The text weaves out of reach most of all for the writer reader.

Lacking celebration calls for the middle voice way.

Metronome music gave up music for me.
I'm irregular if I'm a day.

You can't turn around the same once.
I can't even think what I'm thinking.

Ranger frills. Long range rhyme wills.
Everything encloses something forever.

He said Napoleon said the battle is won or lost in the fold of a map.
Folding doesn't map.

It doesn't even map with itself.
The incredible part is the intentional part.

Intention is by nature inconclusive.
The authority is in the persistence and then falling off.

The author has no right to require belief for right is not conclusively believable.
When you can't hear what is said you feel deprived to the point of indignation.

Listening's commitment to what is heard were an obstacle to further self hearing.
Correctness pauses vitally.

You feel language going in and out of understanding uncaring.
One false mark and I shoot past the mark.

I am not joking because I am not a synonym—
I am the name itself.
Clarice Lispector, *Agua Viva*

Once you start thinking the other way there's no stopping.
You get all caught up without a net.

Close seeing doubles.
The life train is speeding ahead and the fear is getting thrown off like a dangler.

The music is the pulse made audible in the descent.
There's a stillness that haunts excitement down to the toe tips.

It's neither music nor not when leaving the tongue.

"Why don't you get plastic surgery?"
"I want to find out what God wants from this face."

You come to a standstill in the way you are born.
Memory has little need for poetry.

The principle of a thing mates with what it touches.
Inoculate conception.

Confession of a life slave.
Experience is that you go into the place and know it in yourself.

Life's happening on the inside with attached lining.
It's the word that goes feral the moment it leaves your lips.

We are reveling in imperfection to know the possible alive.

If I could cancel the perhaps 34,000 preverbs recorded to date for novelty would I?
An answer here had no relevance to a previous line by the very principle of novelty.
Expect nothing is the poetics.

A poem is a species of language unconcerned with me. Me as merely me.
It has its own ups and downs which make it mine. The mine that is not mine.
Disavowing nothing is the operative poetics.

Nor reaching further than sensing attends in any moment is going by even now.
Language hides from view the facts inside the fact that it is alive.
Its nature is to elude showing knowing its nature. *Stop this*, she says.

It has the same *no being without my being* I have while othering.
It can't lay off the gesture.
It waves its hands speaking on the phone Italian style.

All for my benefit which I can only deny.
It's selling itself as we speak.
It talks with card shark shifty eyes.

Its nature is such that you wouldn't believe it if you knew it.
It's no more believable than poetry and for the same trumped up charges.
It plays charades for the best of causes beyond causation.

It cuts through the middle of the half-way said.
It sucks in its incompletions between syllables half uttered.
This dance is happening nowhere fast.
Its belief is a tune to come.

There's a freedom of saying what no one can claim least of all me.
Poetry animalizes.
Your clown witnesses what you can't bear.

I've been calling on my personal impersona all day so I know she's there.
It's a poem when it is conscious in itself.
At long last a foreigner to myself I begin to speak new.

A line of flight haunts nature at the level of skin.
Personal circumspection rarely extends to mood swings.
A poet is a person complex devoid of self-knowing when not getting any.

I alienate, intransitively speaking.

I want a line like a fish line the free fish makes in flow.
Feel the ripples on the go.
I'm sketching a world from the inside out.

This line is going it knows not where, or how it knows precisely as I don't.
Its truth is not applicable.
I stop reading when attention is not worthy of the book in hand.

The shocking new is just non-recognition with an unrecognizable charge.
Meanwhile the concept ends up in a struggle to represent.
The freest thought doesn't know its author.

Meaning's so now it precedes me.

If the angel of life came to tell you her message would you even notice?
You know you're peaking when the date astonishes.

Can I eat my way out of life?
Dowsing the currents until I hear otherwise.
Life talks back to itself through people, poetry proves.

She suggests dying might be a selfish pleasure.
I feel the spasm that makes you think soul.

Complaint contaminates.

Secretly you make up your mind on the reality status of the invisible.
Listening alters the sound heard.

The read sentence is my new.

Page reading reader tells the poem tale from another way round.
Listening harder hardens sound.

Duende shrieks without complaining.
This report's from behind the stone apparently living again to tell.

I'm plotting the unknowing darkening in the sweat of its brow.
It hardens the core to the core.

Don't know what to do with the mind when things don't line up yet slip through.
Meaning is going up in smoke so we know the fire.

Here I go again unlearning English.
A poem in its patois is calling to its natives.

It's forever spring is a mode of reading faithful in the laying of traps.
It has me by the ankles here on the edge of the bottomless, setting the angle.

The daemon crawling through the syntax scares the semantic before taking hold.
It's taking us too long to catch on, hence the sense of danger, the verbal falling off.

Poetry plots the unknowing subsyntactically.
It starts where thinking completes in the act of itself.

Liberation is sentence by sentence.
The time served.

Some images lose their connection to form at the moment of birth.
My best sketch absents itself along with its objects.

I'm addicted to language rerouting my response before I own it.
When you root through your feet the earth rebounds through your mother organ.

Living in the preverbial now is indescribably infinitely describing.
I found my most individuated moment had less me in it.

All things being equal if and only if they always are, are.
Reading alters the sentence read.

Seeing anything even the page and its moving objects is hands-on.

Seeing is not eating
Hausa proverb

As life is a fatal condition the poem tastes the reader.
No point in complaining about its being in your face.
Why anything reaches across to anything else is linguistic motive still in the dark.

Poetry teaches me I'm an experimental person.
I'm speaking directly but the air between us curves.
Lingualaria trailing keeps trying to get me saying it.

It'll never happen, it never stops to happen.
A vortex passes before you and after.
Who can talk in a place like that, the talking never stops.

Pronouns are feeling a sense of endangerment before turning verb.
It thinks like it rains.
If the sentence had legs they would spread verbaling.

Even thinking light spreads shadows.
The eros of quicksand is a way of mind in the mouth.
When a word hardens over you choke.

Speaking narrowly escapes expelling.
The shape has feel and tonal.
And pastures so to speak speak out flat.

The field is self timing.
You can't think outside it and still be you.
Saying life and then saying death lays bare a gap in the weave to the touch.

No time is like the present.

There is no wisdom not heard. They say this.
Alien tongues have the advantage of surprise.
Wall passage describes how it presses the mind.

The technique is slowing down the background while shredding the foreground.
We seem to be stuck with sensory dodging in the face of text.
The poem shows up offering a manual for seeing through gaps.

Giving up sense and sensibility throws open the corral of the never meant to say.
Or who says among the never known till right now.
Learning to read again starts life all over in an alien tongue.

If it's not strange it's not talking.
The talker through walls is calling you by your remote name.
Can't stop wanting the metanarrative saying all is well in the end.

There's talk aiming to be intransitive.
No freeze, nonsense frees.
Your own drama itself outplays.

Pressure mounting to say a thing is hearing voices.
What's cute is looking the other way when death shows.
No one resists understanding easily.

What poem and death have in common is time neutral.
Anything enters from anywhere at any time—from anytime.

Imagine an entire discourse in your own language you understand not at all.
Call it the drama of the transdramatic or the mind plays intransitive.
I can believe anything now the instant is showing.

Resonant verbal crossflow butterflies from line to line to page between books.
Text boomerangs by the phoneme. Nowhere is safe.
Rogue letters litter the Buddhafields and stay lit.

A line is an eternity surrendering to immediate focus.
We're here because it's endless in our attachment on the move.
I give up consistency to know what consists.

This is literal.
It takes you by the letter.
Conscious art knows like the back of my hand.

Dead talk calls out the exverbial.
I aim to outplay my own drama.
I'm addressing my failures to refer.

But it's getting away as I speak.
Anything from anywhere anytime and further.
The subtext is transtensing.

The idea is time neutral.
It's willing to talk itself into the ground.
Everything goes both ways without noticing.
The end is where it stops getting out of itself.

The longing into eternity lines any moment dead center.
Never having said it sources.

Inability speaks exceedingly.
Mind lives from the middle out.
To know it through means speaking recombinant.

No can do has raga.
Neutral never neuters.
It takes effect over time.

Knowing true is a matter of ear.
Wandering page after page wondering.
I keep my eye on the blank spaces with a wink.

Her life or her poem holds together by resurgent (re)quest.
The hand won't stay still says dakini shows writative.
It's only language for the moment.

Her poem carries on by asking.
She heals so to speak by the lighted finger within the page.
Things happening raise impossible questions no one notices and then do.

Meaning is the pulse cresting in your mind on paper.
Her spasm that makes the soul seek words images truth.
We've heard this before as we go before verbs right now.

The daemon's between the details.

He had a way of talking, 'twas a language all his own,
Life's story, love and glory if you listen when he plays it for you
Rashaan Roland Kirk

Exhaust the vehicle before it exhausts you.
Knowing nothing progresses things progress knowingly.

By what measure her freedom of mind but I fail before you.

I know the art knows me like the back of my hand, which I recall never.
A good sentence loses you before in the end you are found.
Effect is an artifact of sounding at home.

I don't speak koan unless it speak me first.
I'm over educated and under informed.
Unless these words get jammed back together, truth sails freer.

We keep meeting like this like there's no other way but no tomorrow.
The instrument crashes that mere memory burn.
It's hard not deciding.

Text the receiver proves porous selves.
Intransigence intransitizes awkwardly.
Anything verbs when verbally.

Grammar puts out in hiding.
Love text is subtext of own text. (Theorem I)
Getting fiddled in hindsight is insightful joyously.

I never get used to how hard she talks.
Letting now go now.

*The multiverse wants to make love to itself through us
but we fail to grasp the terms of engagement.*
Ontononymous the Particular

For most of life dying is what other people do. Then not.

Truth is unknown to itself but it knows its voice.
Words are trying to pull apart serving their sentence.
I pull back the lens in time.

Working on the inside here, bare labials, I'm reminded.
Unwinding is dire dancing. Think dying.
Language is a monumentally unthinkable fact.

The word uses up the thought for the moment; then stores it away.
It gets my mind off the hook. No stories apply.
It converts to magic by releasing its intrinsic ability to change what it touches.

Dance acknowledges there's nowhere to go.
Poem matches as spur for bounce back.
A line is a vein.

The poem makes me strange to myself.
Duende surges through the friction of letters.
It scorches time until it yields to outside.

Ravaging time teaches inexorable living.
The poem goes against nature as nature wants.
Metaphor faithfully drags into view the incommensurable beloved.

It comes to resolve no resolution.

I long ago gave up thinking here.
How can I say this but do anyway.
I even try to cling to what I can't think.

This is an ancient conversation, I wasn't invited, dimly overhearing.

Others will have said this before me by the nature of misunderstood thought.
Poetry imitates nature in its mode of operation by going against.
I write the thing so it can turn strange and forget me.

Compelling this conversation (that) never knows where it's going.
Modal verbs might talk roots in every sound breath.

No can do this breathing timely immemorial.
Imposing my thought on the word it sounds pain.
I don't understand my own prolepsis and can that word even mean who knows.

When I hear voices I think it's only things.
The conversation stretches around the globe and presently.
Imagine every word charged with meaning everything ever not said. History.

Biodiverse is verse with a future in hand. Read my fortune.
Sentencing the world is word order cutting through.
It pulls roots up and higher it goes.

You are already my future mind if you've come this far without me.
Babel is a modal reality stretching syntax from within.
It can't be liked. It likes for itself.

There is a point in any utterance when it flashes empty: no change necessary.
We sit around waiting for the world mind talking back.
Syntax hides its own parting of the waters.

I'm not from your tribe, so I'm making this map.
Undertime undermind retains our waiting.
Attitudes find nowhere to sit.

Do real things come out of the woodwork?
What lives inside this question?
Believing in what you say is a reach around the back of the actual words.

We're trying to stay in contact as the winds are pulling us apart.
Writing about dying requires dying inside language in equivalence.
Poetry makes certainty undesirable.

A word actively engaged is not mainly signifier but matrix nodally happening.
Reinvent restart. You never know when it will get to you.
Get close enough and you turn multiple.

Nothing oversaid, nothing to unsay.
The poem creates a big enough surface tangle we find our way by unsafe means.
Not getting lost on the inside requires reading signs of the invisible referent.

All your ducks in a row trips up orientation so scramble.
Read the poem barefooted.

Get lost.

Welcome, I give you a world I don't know.

Being contrary likens to seeing a star cart is both ways at once.
The sorcerer's text embodies knowing knowing itself in the way it knows you.
Stand clear or else.

The rider is giving the only kind that can never be given so as to be taken.
A function of my cherished statement's little more than moving us along the edge.
Poetry distracts us from vertigo.

It's coming in time which can mean not at all.

The text is true when every reading of the same differs.
Looking actual identity in the eyes shakes the foundation.
You recognize the unrecognizable and lay back relieved.

No attempt to reach the other side matches it's coming to you as rite of passage.
Time is disappearing you, you have to laugh.
Mind is not minding but I do mind.

Intuition is truer surviving counterintuitive thinking.
Incursion is unexpected by nature.
Mind on drift dumbs down to average the response.

Putting one foot after the other knows the earth flat.
All the world in a line swirls the given spacetime timely.

The poem is touching as with fingers reaching out of a hole in planet earth.

The forest collaborates by mood.

May be necessary to hold back from buddhahood as flesh comes to flesh, traction.

Subvisible light suffuses by the aperture subfuse.

A word means what it says so read mind first.

Living in mind enters appearance through linguality.

That brings us *here*. Word or not.

In poetry life is at stake in that death is.

Mind is not mind that minds minding like this.

Just checking in to see what's offered.

It's only suspect when it aims to please.

It cracks heads like eggs.

The poet is the last mind bending.

The line starting life over is not poetry beyond beyond.

The referents may hide but we can't help smelling them.

Hope is no one and nothing minds.

The vehicle is not moving but it goes both ways at once.

Duende can't sit still.

Think shaman whose day job is private eye.

Life staked, blue dagger, tent flaps flying, can't stop crying.

I say I am the sacrifice here when I can say I is.

She wants me worn through so she shows thread bare.

My daemon likes me better at the end of my tether: zero resistance.
Tamped down to the stub of memory no choice but life flows its first force by me.
Call the indelible poem to show residual recall of self-stalking.

A moving space open on both ends is receptive to absurdity.
The fine line you walk between art and trickery is the plank.
We become what we withhold.

I discover acting with unreasonable reason. See Spot run.
Reading being impossible made me impossible.
We become what we extol. We're instantly out of fashion.

Unresolvable difference is mainstream.
Racism is a subcategory of otherism.
So here we're hacking away for a poetics of self-stalking.

I'm trying to take being tricked as a gift.
Language stirs in the nether.
This is a space of like it or not anything is said and not for me to say.

Assemblage please a little to the right.
Prime singularity has no peer, no fear.
Self-destruction is non-functioning here in the bright nowhere.

The true tricker self-tricks before you.
Look for a readerly poetics of lifting your disguise midway in the sentence. Too late.

Bye bye buddha guise. Boils are just for show.

The variant human never stands before you.
The many worlds theory tells us we're unknown beyond the wildest imagination.
Suddenly you almost can't resist going outside and screaming once for all time.

Alternatively ask nicely before absolute action.
It's not in the words, maybe it's between them, but I feel surrounded.
Place presumes.

Words are hard when given their proper place adamantine.
The words I don't know must have forgotten me.
It is by such logic that teachers trick you.

All important is being polite asking for the impossible.
The no ruckus request tracks cosmos in its rare clear mood.
Didactic jokes have alchemy on their bad breath.

How otherwise get to our lost others but through their death?
Last breath best breath means now or not.
Making progress in the place of no progression.

Predicate likeness by speaking to yourself through your own death.
Sooner or later all lines point to an actual center that goes where you go.
Never going on display is the upside of the wing on its way.

Raga replays never same.
Rereading the page is an altered state happening.
You half remember the path of almost unbearable bliss.

No remedy for studying nature in my dance steps.
She knows the poem real is taking you over the edge.

Not quick enough to catch my act I fall through the cracks.
Outsourcing is playing out with hands open.

Some teachers turn tricks for prophets.
The problem with first thought best thought is how first means.

Not to translate the non-human but to serve being its resonance.
It gets me nowhere where no is not.

Place consumes to resume.
Uncertainty never goes away.

Act true like an angle.
Not noticing puts you on notice in time.

Symbols are unreliable in empty hands.
Nothing is beautiful but it teach unrequesting.

We fall into shape.
Never not thinking dying.

Poem flies with a dying rise.
The daemon smiles demise.

Self generating terms of engagement happy to incomprehend beyond belief.

The smile inspires the poem separating from its properties.
This is putting my writerly Cheshire othering on notice, performatively speaking.

Writing daily to know who I am now. Shazam!
Honor the longshot head held high still above water poetics.
Poem creates reader.

Thinking discovers it wants outside itself enough to seek a bypass.
Every line an *ars poetica*.
It talks about itself to liberate me from talking about myself.

Death aspires to be the matrix of beauty.
The threshold between living and dying hides the limen of artifice and nature.
Heightened states know my two arms, two eyes, two brains, two tongues one wave.

I cross waving.
Poet and reader have parity variably.

Particular is anywhere anytime anything whatever wherever is or not itself.
Balance is being on the right side without loss of wrong side.

Quanta falling stick around with no need of crossing, poetically speaking.
Duende stirs the midpoint at both ends.
The poem is the other to another we are neither of now.

Soma the body between shows up eaten by the end and therefore here at last.
Like likens like to like and unlike alike.
The hole in the whole is the heaven within hearing.

Contents by Poem Title

anteroom: the first house

alternate lingualities

every sound its word

the eros of soft exterior shocks

sound talk

eternal discomfort of the heavenly bent

not even rabbits go down this hole

About the Author

GEORGE QUASHA is a poet, artist, writer, and musician working in mediums in which he explores certain principles active within composition. His primary medium is language, but principles discovered there are operative also in sculpture, drawing, video, sound, and performance. He has published some thirty books, a selection of which is listed in the front of the book.

His ongoing video work, for which he was awarded a Guggenheim Fellowship (2006), **art is/music is/poetry is (Speaking Portraits)**, has recorded over a thousand artists, poets, and composers (in eleven countries) saying what in their view art, music, or poetry is. Nine volumes of the work appear currently at www.art-is-international.org. Exhibitions of this and axial drawings and paintings include the Snite Museum of Art (University of Notre Dame), White Box (NYC), the Samuel Dorsky Museum (SUNY New Paltz), and biennials (Wroclaw, Poland; Geneva, Switzerland; Kingston, New York).

He lives in Barrytown, New York, where he collaborates with Susan Quasha in making art and books, and together they publish Station Hill Press.